ELVIS: TRUT

An Intimate Conv...
Elvis Presley's Closest Friend and Confidant

As told to L.E. McCullough
& Harold F. Eggers, Jr.

Jan 23, 2020

Troy,

Music, film & innovation is in your heart & spirit. a wonder to Behold. God Bless you my friend.

Harold F. Eggers Jr.

ELVIS: TRUTH, MYTH & BEYOND

An Intimate Conversation with Lamar Fike, Elvis Presley's Closest Friend and Confidant

As told to L.E. McCullough
& Harold F. Eggers, Jr.

Hound Dog Books & Media LLC
P.O. Box 352, Woodbridge NJ 07095

© 2016 L.E. McCullough, Harold F. Eggers, Jr. & Lamar Fike

First Printing: August, 2016

ISBN 978-0-9967889-0-8 (eBook)
ISBN 978-0-9967889-1-5 (softcover)
ISBN 978-0-9967889-2-2 (hardcover)

Front & back cover design by David Simpson Design LLC
www.davidsimpsondesignllc.com

400 QUESTIONS

You Always Wanted to Ask

about ELVIS ...

NEARLY 40 YEARS after his death, Elvis Presley remains one of the most intriguing human beings of the last century.

Millions of people still want to know intimate details of Elvis' life:

What did he think about his music?

What did he really do behind the gates of Graceland?

What were his final thoughts the day he died?

We have the answers here.

* * *

Does the world need yet another book about Elvis?

Perhaps not.

But it will want **Elvis: Truth, Myth & Beyond.**

Because it is Real.

* * *

Elvis: Truth, Myth & Beyond is not a gushy fan tribute.

It is not a dry recitation of facts.

It is not a pop-psych portrait by an envious outsider.

It is <u>exactly</u> what the title states: personal, direct statements concerning the truth and myth of Elvis Presley as told by the one friend Elvis never was able to turn away.

* * *

Until *Elvis: Truth, Myth & Beyond*, Lamar Fike never had the chance to tell the full story — one-on-one — of his remarkable friendship with the world's greatest music star.

Elvis: Truth, Myth & Beyond — 400 questions, and as much truth about Elvis as you're ready to handle.

Are you ready?

* * *

ELVIS: TRUTH, MYTH & BEYOND

An Intimate Conversation with Lamar Fike, Elvis Presley's Closest Friend and Confidant

~ <u>CONTENTS</u> ~

~ **Foreword by Marty Lacker** ~

WHOEVER COINED the phrase "He was one of a kind" certainly had Lamar Fike in mind.

Lamar was so many things, and they were all good.

He was a good friend, intelligent, talented and one of the wittiest people you'd ever meet.

Marty Lacker
(photo courtesy Marty Lacker)

He was known for his Lamarisms, and they were doozies, sharp and to the point; he could almost be crowned as the "comeback kid".

He and Elvis were like brothers, and what brought him even closer to Elvis is the fact that Lamar knew and was close to Elvis' mother, whereas only a couple of other of The Memphis Mafia knew her.

He was her favorite of all those around Elvis, and that connected him and Elvis forever.

Lamar had a good heart, and he lived up to the saying, "A friend in need is a friend indeed." If you were his friend, if he had something and you needed it, it was yours.

Lamar was like a brother to me, and it greatly saddened me when he left us after battling his illness for his last years.

My life is better because of my brother Lamar. May he Rest In Peace.

* * *

— *Marty Lacker is an original member of The Memphis Mafia and author with Patsy Lacker and Leslie B. Smith of* **Elvis, Portrait of a Friend.**

~ **Introduction** ~

"Before Elvis there was nothing." — *John Lennon*

———————————

Elvis **Aaron Presley**, an American singer and actor born in the most humble and ordinary of socio-economic circumstances, spent the last 23 years of his relatively short life setting the world on fire.

His unique musical taste and performance style not only transformed the popular music of his day but sparked a massive revolution in popular culture that reached every part of the planet.

From July 7, 1954 — when his first record was played over local radio — to the moment you are reading this, someone somewhere has been thinking, talking or dreaming about Elvis every single day.

One snapshot in time, the Harris Poll® of August 12, 2002, discovered that 84% of adult Americans (176 million) claimed their lives were touched in some way by Elvis Presley — watching a movie starring Elvis (70%), dancing to an Elvis song (44%), viewing a movie or television program about Elvis (42%).

Nearly 40 years after his death, Elvis continues to exist in almost every segment of contemporary culture via thousands of visual images, literary references, jokes about Elvis sightings.

There are Elvis impersonators, Elvis postage stamps, uncountable millions of individual Elvis knick-knacks … a continuing stream of newly packaged Elvis recordings and videos are disseminated through every type of broadcast media every minute of every hour.

There are Elvis shrines, Elvis religious cults, Elvis museums, Elvis holograms.

And a seemingly endless parade of Elvis books, just like this one.

This Elvis book is different.

It contains 41,000 words about Elvis spoken by a man who knew Elvis before <u>and</u> after he became an icon, a commodity, a legend.

It is a book of intimate recollections from a 23-year friendship that attempts to answer a single question: **what was it like to be Elvis?**

Though virtually every public moment of his life has been documented, Elvis himself left no memoir, no diary, no revealing personal correspondence. The essence of his true personality will always be glimpsed through the refracted insights of his associates, friends and family members.

Some of the most brilliant and tantalizing insights about Elvis have come to us through a man named **Lamar Fike**.

Lamar's connection with Elvis dated from early 1954 (just before Elvis' first history-making Sun records) until the day Elvis died in 1977. Lamar was there for the entire ride: Hollywood, the Army, Las Vegas and everything in-between.

He was a charter member of Presley's famed "Memphis Mafia", the tight-knit group of friends and personal assistants who protected and sustained Elvis as his career ebbed and flowed.

In fact, Lamar lived with Elvis and his family <u>before</u> Elvis became The King of Rock 'n' Roll; he was very much the "brother" figure Elvis sought throughout his life.

Until his death on January 21, 2011, Lamar Fike remained the close friend and confidant whose recollections offer the greatest genuine insight into the complex character of a man who irreversibly changed 20th-century musical and cultural history.

In September, 2001, *Elvis: Truth, Myth & Beyond* authors L.E. McCullough and Harold F. Eggers, Jr. were invited by Lamar Fike to conduct an intensive two-day interview at his home in Nashville, Tennessee.

Lamar fielded hundreds of questions about Elvis with clarity and conciseness; the marathon Q. and A. yielded a plethora of never-before-told insights into what made Elvis tick.

In conversations with the authors over the ensuing years, Lamar made it emphatically clear that he wanted *Elvis: Truth, Myth & Beyond* to present and preserve as much "real truth" about Elvis as possible.

Turns out a lot of that Real Truth about Elvis can be found in the parallel life of Lamar Fike.

* * *

Lamar Rielly Fike was born November 11, 1935, the first child of James Lamar Fike (1910-54) and Margaret Rielly Fike (1911-94). Like Elvis, Lamar was a native of smalltown Mississippi — Cleveland, located a hundred miles south of Memphis on U.S. Route 61, a highway made famous in the lyrics of numerous Delta blues singers and folkrock balladeer Bob Dylan.

Lamar's parents had both been born and raised in the small Central Texas town of Mart, 25 miles east of Waco. James Fike's father, James Benjamin Fike, had migrated there from Alabama in 1901 and married Mary Magdelene Sansom from nearby Oletha, Texas, in 1905. Margaret Fike's parents, Thomas Rielly and Margaret Jane Miller Rielly, had settled in Mart when Thomas was hired as a conductor for the Missouri Pacific Railroad, which counted Mart as one of its route hubs.

After years as a successful farm implement salesman throughout West Central Mississippi, James Fike started his own company selling army surplus in 1945. He moved the family, which now included Lamar's younger sister Mary Jane born in 1940, to Memphis, three years before the Presley family arrived in the Bluff City from Tupelo.

As a boy, Lamar was intrigued by music and music business, singing in the choir at St. John's Episcopal Church in Memphis and arranging bookings for local bands when he was only 14.

"I would sell the bands all over, from colleges to car lots," he recalled. "One summer I think I made more money than my dad."

Lamar's sister Mary Jane concurs. "Lamar was a born promoter," she says. "From a young age, Lamar had the skills and personality required to live the life of celebrity."

Lamar's early show business stirrings often rendered the budding impresario restless. "I was the type of person who stared out the window in class, always thinking about something else. The teachers said I had the greatest intelligence they had ever seen, but I never used it on schoolwork. I saw myself doing something else, and I always liked the entertainment business. My dream at the time was to be a radio deejay."

The life paths of Elvis and Lamar first conjoined in early 1954 at Sam Phillips' Memphis Recording Service/Sun Recording Studio. Lamar was learning the fine points of audio engineering, Elvis was struggling to express the innovative musical ideas jelling in his mind.

By 1957, their young lives would be linked forever when Elvis — now a national entertainment sensation — invited the freshly unemployed Lamar to drive to Los Angeles and hang out during a movie shoot.

Asked what he did during his years with Elvis, Lamar's reply was simple and without the least degree of pretension: "Everything."

Through two decades of daily business operations, Lamar came to play a primary role in every aspect of presenting Elvis Presley to the public.

- He assisted on Elvis' movie sets, designed and ran lights and sound at Elvis' concerts, served as a bodyguard and driver for Elvis' tours and personal trips.

- When Elvis was drafted into the U.S. Army and sent to Fort Hood and then West Germany, Lamar accompanied him, making sure the world's hottest music star could maintain some degree of stateside normalcy.

- As manager of Elvis' Nashville-based publishing company, Hill & Range, from 1963-72, Lamar scouted and pitched songs for Elvis' recording sessions; many of those songs became monster hits.

- Lamar worked with Elvis' manager, Colonel Parker, as part of the advance team setting up Elvis' tours; when Elvis began performing in Las Vegas, Lamar assumed duty as his lighting designer/director.

- Lamar's involvement in Elvis' personal life was equally as intense. As detailed in this book, Lamar actively participated in the impulsive, often reckless lifestyle of a celebrity who was for all intents and purposes a law unto himself. "We never grew up," Lamar reflected. "We never had to."

But the most important role Lamar Fike played in the life of Elvis Presley was that of Friend. It was a friendship born not of happenstance but forged from a deeper destiny.

* * *

During 1957-58 Lamar lived with Elvis and his parents at Graceland and became intimately aware of the complex family history and psychological dynamics that would influence Elvis until his final hour.

"We knew what each other was thinking," said Lamar of his longstanding mental affinity with Elvis. "Brothers are that way. Twins are that way. We were that way."

Tommy McDonald, currently of Arlington, Texas, was Lamar's first cousin and grew up in Mart. As children, the two developed a lifelong bond reinforced by frequent family visits during summer vacation and Christmas. Affirms Tommy, "Lamar never had a job that he liked until he got with Elvis."

12

Tommy first met Elvis in 1958 when Lamar called him to come to Fort Hood after the funeral of Elvis' mother Gladys in Memphis. In addition to Elvis, Tommy met the singer's grandmother Minnie Mae Presley, father Vernon Presley, then girlfriend Anita Wood and high school buddy Red West.

It was clear, says Tommy, that Lamar had been accepted by Elvis' mother, Gladys, as a virtual Presley family member. "I personally think that Gladys looked on Lamar as an embodiment of her other son, Jesse Garon, Elvis' twin who had died at birth," he avers.

Following Elvis' death, Lamar immersed himself in the commercial music industry, making full use of the organizational skills he had refined during two decades of collaboration with the world's biggest music star.

Recalls Tommy McDonald, "Shortly after the funeral, Lamar called me where I was living in Arlington, Texas, and said, 'I'm going to start a management company here in Nashville. Can you come and help me run things? You're a lot better at details than I am.' I said, 'Well, allright, I will', and for three years I helped him operate Lamar Fike Management."

The company managed several country and pop music acts including Billy Joe Shaver, Townes Van Zandt, Henson Cargill, Little David Wilkins, Sunday Sharpe, Billie Joe Spears, Ray Pillow and Bill Sparkman and also operated a booking agency and two music publishing companies, created radio and television programs featuring country music headliners and served as a consultant for music publishers and record producers.

Recording executive Kevin Eggers, whose music business career began as a co-producer with promoter Sid Bernstein of the first Beatles and Rolling Stones U.S. tours and went on to include his own groundbreaking Poppy and Tomato record labels, knew Lamar from the early 1960s and worked with him on numerous projects over a 30-year period.

"Lamar was regarded as a kingpin in Nashville," says Eggers. "Lamar dealt with everybody on the highest level — the Who's Who of songwriters from Johnny Cash and Doc Pomus to Burt

Bacharach and Jacques Brel. Everyone wanted to get their songs to Elvis, and Lamar was the gatekeeper."

And he was uniquely suited for the responsibility.

"Lamar had a great ear," Eggers states. "He was a very sophisticated music person and enjoyed all types of music, not just rock or country. He could hear a hit song a mile away."

A selection of song demos would be prepared at the Hill & Range office in New York, says Eggers, and then delivered to Nashville for Lamar to give a first listen. Elvis would come to the Nashville office after hours, and he and Lamar would play and discuss the possibilities, eventually picking out what Elvis wanted to record for his upcoming album.

"That kind of creative relationship is so important," notes Eggers. "Elvis trusted Lamar completely. Lamar had complete access to Elvis on the most intimate level. At one time Lamar had, I think, four or five songs on the charts at the same time."

Besides his business acumen, Lamar exhibited an unflagging penchant for boosting the careers of others.

As 1977 rolled around, Lamar had come to believe strongly in the hit-making potential of songwriter/performer Little David Wilkins and chose a dozen Little David songs for Elvis to consider for his next album. Elvis selected five songs and invited Little David to come to the album recording session set for Graceland following Elvis' return from his Fall tour. Tragically, this collaboration never came to pass.

Pat Rolfe, who retired in 2010 as Vice President of ASCAP (American Society of Composers, Authors and Publishers), worked as Lamar's secretary at Hill & Range from 1966-1972. "If it weren't for Lamar," she avows, "I wouldn't have had my career in publishing."

Lamar never failed to go the extra mile for his clients, says Rolfe. "If one of our writers had a song we knew was a good song but wasn't going to be a big hit on the radio or sell a lot of records,

Lamar would work to get it into one of Elvis' movies and onto an Elvis soundtrack album. This would draw royalties from around the world for years. He would help his writers anyway he could, help them pay their bills and feed their family. That was important to Lamar."

From 1989-95, Lamar worked as a collaborator to Capitol Records Nashville executive Jimmy Bowen, an award-winning producer who shaped the recording success of artists like Frank Sinatra, Dean Martin, Sammy Davis, Jr., Reba McEntire, George Strait, Garth Brooks, Glen Campbell and more. Bowen says his transition to country music from rock and pop got a big boost from Lamar's friendship and assistance.

"Lamar helped me get introduced to Nashville, get to know the lay of the land on Music Row, so to speak. The country music industry was a very small circle of movers and shakers back then; maybe a dozen people or so controlled what happened. Lamar was a great help knowing who was connected to who."

Lamar operated Bowen's publishing company and had, says Bowen, few equals in terms of working knowledge of the intricacies of the music publishing business. "He understood the entire process, and he was great working with writers. Lamar really knew songs. He instinctively knew what song would be good for what artist."

Eddie Kilroy, past president of Playboy Records and producer of numerous hits by Jerry Lee Lewis, Mickey Gilley and Marty Robbins, believes Lamar honed those instincts during his years with Elvis.

"Deep down, he was preparing himself for the day when Elvis was gone, whether Elvis would quit the music industry or die or whatever," Kilroy says. "By learning other aspects of the business, Lamar was preparing for the future."

Lamar also made conscientious efforts to chronicle and clarify the past.

Shortly after Elvis' death, Lamar signed on to serve as a consultant for what would, unfortunately, turn out to be a controversial and much-criticized biography — *Elvis* by Albert Goldman, published in 1981.

Before the book went to press, Lamar was not given the chance to review the final galleys and correct numerous factual errors. After publication, he was so repulsed by the book's inaccuracies that he disassociated himself entirely from the project.

In 1994, Lamar contributed a foreword and extensive background for *The Elvis Encyclopedia* by David E. Stanley and Frank Coffey; the following year, he participated in interviews for *Elvis Aaron Presley: Revelations from the Memphis Mafia* by Alanna Nash.

He also appeared in several film and television documentaries including *Life with Elvis* (1991), *All the King's Men* (1997), *Mr. Rock & Roll: Colonel Tom Parker* (1999), *The Elvis Mob* (2004) and Martin Scorsese's documentary on Bob Dylan, *No Direction Home: Bob Dylan* (2005).

During his final years Lamar was eagerly sought as an authoritative source of Elvis information, participating in a globe-spanning circuit of television shows, lectures, symposia, collector conventions and fan fairs.

In October, 2010, Lamar was admitted to Arlington Memorial Hospital. From the day he checked in to the day he passed away, his cousin Tommy McDonald was at his side.

"I was there at the end," recalls Tommy. "Two days before his death, he told me, 'Tommy you have to promise me faithfully that you will see to it that Harold and L.E.'s book will be published so that everyone will know the true story.'"

In his final moments, says Tommy, "he was smiling, really smiling. I asked him, 'What or who do you see?' He just closed his eyes, still smiling.'"

Lamar Fike died January 21, 2011. He was cremated and his headstone marker placed in the Fike family plot at Mart Cemetery.

The authors of *Elvis: Truth, Myth & Beyond* are grateful for the guidance he gave during his final months as they finished this book.

Though Lamar would grow up to travel the world and move among the highest levels of celebrity, it was perhaps inevitable that Mart, Texas, would be his final earthly resting place.

"Mart was your typical small town," he once said. "Just a sleepy, quiet little Texas town. When we would visit there as kids, everybody knew me and I knew them. I thought that when you died, you went to Mart instead of Heaven."

* * *

What will you learn about Elvis from these 400 questions answered by Lamar Fike?

First, that it took guts to be Elvis.

As bizarre as today's Elvis impersonators might appear to current audiences, imagine the mental pressure cooker the Real Elvis endured as he underwent the sometimes rapturous, sometimes strained metamorphosis of an average face-in-the-crowd Memphis teenager into The King of Rock 'n' Roll.

Number Two, that being Elvis required the dedicated help and support of a close circle of friends and family who believed in him. As a performer. As a person.

Lamar Fike was one of those friends.

Sit down here a while, and he'll tell you about the Elvis Presley you thought you already knew. At the peak of his popularity. At the depth of his despair.

You'll also learn about that little bit of Elvis we carry around inside, each and every one of us. Elvis may have left the building, but his voice is still in our soul.

Lamar Fike
(photo courtesy Estate of Lamar Fike)

For a gallery of fan and press photos depicting the friendship
of Elvis Presley and Lamar Fike through the years,
go to **www.pinterest.com** and search:
"Elvis and Lamar"

~ **Family Roots: The Boy in the Man** ~

- Elvis Aaron Presley is born January 8, 1935, to Vernon and Gladys Presley in the poorest section of Tupelo, Mississippi; a twin brother, Jesse Garon, is stillborn.

- As a child, Elvis regularly attends Assembly of God services with his mother and is introduced to the church's ecstatic style of gospel music and dance.

- May, 1938: Vernon Presley is sentenced to three years in Mississippi state prison for check forgery; Elvis and Gladys go on public assistance.

- During the early 1940s, Elvis is enthralled by radio broadcasts of country, blues and swing music.

- May, 1944: Elvis makes first of several appearances on radio station WELO's *Black and White Jamboree* with country guitarist Mississippi Slim; the next year, Elvis wins a $5 prize in a county fair talent contest singing *Old Shep*.

- November, 1948: the Presleys move to Memphis, Tennessee; when Elvis' voice changes, he thinks he has become possessed by the devil.

- August 14, 1958: Gladys Presley dies of heart failure, age 46; Elvis receives more than 100,000 sympathy cards and letters.

- July 3, 1960, Vernon remarries; dies June 26, 1979 of heart failure and is buried next to wife Gladys and sons Jesse and Elvis.

Q. Did Elvis ever talk of his childhood?

A. Not a lot, but every once in a while, he would. He didn't have a lot of fond memories of his childhood.

Q. Did he resent his father for going to jail?

A.   He never talked about it. None of that came up. Elvis just didn't talk about it that much. Just something he didn't talk about.

Q. Did Gladys try to protect him from the world?

A.   Absolutely. Always. She was a good, kind, generous person. Gladys would give you the blouse off her back. That's just the way she was. Everybody in the family loved Gladys, because she took care of everybody. Gladys was the matriarch of that whole family. I mean, everybody leaned toward Gladys. Everybody did.

Q. What about Vernon?

A.   Vernon was always distrustful of everybody. I think prison made it worse. Vernon didn't like anybody. Vernon liked me. He marginally liked me. But Vernon, he always felt everybody was a threat to him. We got along real well. In fact, I was the only one in the group to call him Vernon. Never called him Mr. Presley. Everybody else called him Mr. Presley. I always called him Vernon. He was afraid people would try to separate him from Elvis. And he worried how the money was spent and stuff like that, you know.

Q. Did Gladys protect you? When Elvis got ornery, would she step in and say, "Elvis—"

A. Yeah, she would. She'd say to him, "Calm down. Leave him alone." He would do it. We'd get in an argument or something, and she saw that he started it, and she'd say, "Now, you need to stop that. That's enough of that." And Elvis would say, "Well, Momma…" "No, there's no Momma to it. You need to stop that." And later on, he'd say to me, "Listen, you son of a bitch…" And I said, "You know better than to start it in front of your mother. You know how she is." Gladys really liked me, and I liked Gladys. I genuinely liked Gladys. I really, really liked her, and she knew it.

Q. What was it like when Elvis argued back to Gladys?

A. The biggest fights that Elvis had were with his mother. Vernon talked real low. Gladys screamed at the top of her lungs. You could hear her in the next county. They used to get in fights at the table. The big fights happened at the dinner table or the breakfast table. And boy, I mean, it scared the shit out of me. Elvis and her would start arguing, and God Almighty, you had to get out of the room. I mean, it got so loud. They'd throw food at each other and stuff like that. It got really bad, yeah.

Elvis had his mother's temper. Elvis was exactly like his mother. They were like two peas in a pod. And the temper tantrums would just be horrendous. When I was living at the house in 1957, I mean, I was in the line of fire every day. It was just rough. You couldn't get away.

Q. Was she ever angry outside the home?

A. When she was young, Gladys was out in the field one time working as a field hand. This guy that owned this place was on a horse, came up to her, got off the horse, started arguing with her. She picked up a plow share. You know what a plow share is? Plow share weighs 75-100 pounds. Picked it up, hit him right between the eyes with it and damn near killed him. She was strong as an ox. She was very strong. Big woman. That's where Elvis got his wide shoulders, from her, not his father. Gladys had these big, wide shoulders. That's where Elvis got it, from Gladys. Elvis' looks were from Gladys. That dark hair and that skin and everything. The dark eyes also.

But Gladys' anger came from fear. She was scared. Gladys was reacting out of fear. Fear that he would be hurt. She was always scared of that. She always said she could never stand to see Elvis or Vernon in the grave. Couldn't stand to see it. That was her wish. So that's the reason she died like she did.

Q. Was Gladys frightened by Elvis' sudden fame?

A. The fame was moving real fast. They would get in a car, Gladys and Vernon, and drive around in that pink Cadillac or whatever. Gladys would dip snuff. Carried a little Maxwell House can to spit in. Everybody in town recognized them. That bothered her. It really bothered her.

Elvis' fame, I think, had more to do with Gladys' death than anything. It just worried her to death. She was a chronic worrier. She worried all the time. Her drinking caused a lot of it, too. You know, he was an only child. I mean, here's a woman that would follow him to school, walk him to school. When he was in 10th-11th grade, she'd walk him to school. You're talking serious shit here. You're not talking lightweight stuff. Elvis was a momma's boy. There was no if, ands, buts. He was a momma's boy. I mean, he was. That was it. Elvis could do no wrong around Gladys — ever.

She never let him grow. She just suffocated Elvis. It'd drive Elvis crazy. Later on he toughened up. Everything Elvis did was for his mother. When he lost her, it was a void that was never filled. No. She was the matriarchal head of that house. It was a matriarchal family. Most families would be patriarchal, but she was the real and symbolic center of the house. When she died, Elvis became the center.

Q. Was Gladys a religious woman?

A. When Elvis was younger, yeah. Latter years, she never went to church. But she was a very religious woman. Had a lot of superstitions. That's that odd thing growing up in the South, where you find superstitions right next to hard-core religious belief. She passed that superstitious attitude to her son. Elvis was superstitious as hell. Just little things would happen. She'd tell him to watch out for this. Gladys didn't trust anybody. That's where Elvis got it. He didn't trust anybody, either.

Q. What role did Vernon play at the time?

A. Vernon never became the center of the house. Never, ever. I mean, Vernon worked for his son. So I mean, you know, you can imagine what kind of transitional situation that was. You couldn't tell Elvis what to do. You've got a son making $10 million a year.

In fact, Elvis fired him one day. They called me. I was in the kitchen. Vernon said, "You need to come up here." I said, "What is it?" He said, "Come on up here." So I started coming up the steps, and Vernon came by me, and I said, "What's going on?" He said, "Elvis just fired me." I said, "Shit. I ain't got a chance. I know that I'm next."

I walked in the room. I said, "Am I next?" He said, "What do you mean?" I said, "Well, you just fired your daddy. God Almighty, there ain't nothing between you and me and him."

He said, "No, I'm not gonna fire Daddy. I just told him that."

But I mean, stuff like that went on. Those were fights. I mean, how often is it you fire your father? Guy's 22 years old firing his father.

Q. Was it a huge shock for Vernon to see his son become an international music and film star?

A. It was unbelievable. It used to drive Vernon nuts — all the guys around Elvis, the whole entourage — because Vernon thought they were spending his money. He didn't like that. Vernon had a backache a long, long time. Vernon never really was a big provider. Gladys was the provider. It was a strictly matriarchal family. It was not a patriarchal family. It was all matriarchal. I mean, tight as it was, that's what it was. It was Gladys, then Elvis, then Vernon. She ran it all. She was the provider. Vernon was not. She was. And he was taken out of the role immediately when Elvis became a star.

Q. Did Elvis feel close to his dad at all?

A. He was very close to his dad. Loved his dad big time. But, you know, he would get into arguments with him all the time. He respected his father. But he didn't particularly. He had a hard time when his dad remarried. But he handled it.

Q. How did Elvis' extended family regard him?

A. He was somebody to borrow money from. He took care of all of them. Took care of everybody in that family. They borrowed money from him all the time. He'd always give them money.

Q. Did they have any idea what a great musical innovator he was?

A. Oh, yeah, they knew.

Q. Were they proud of him?

A. Absolutely. Super proud, yeah. When you look at it, there was nobody like him. It was the first time an ordinary American teenager from out of nowhere became a household word everywhere in the world.

Q. Did Elvis have a lot of relatives on the payroll?

A. Not toward the end, they weren't at all. He got rid of all his relatives, outside of people that worked there at Graceland. He didn't have to put up with them, because they didn't see him.

Q. Gladys and Vernon had moved to Killeen, Texas, to be with Elvis during basic training at Fort Hood?

A. That's right. Elvis rented a house from the local mayor. Gladys and Vernon came down and moved into the house with us. Elvis had a white '58 Fleetwood Cadillac, and they drove that down from Memphis with a trailer on the back of it, little small trailer.

Q. How long after moving to Killeen did Gladys become ill?

A. They moved in late June, and shortly after, she began to get sick. She was getting sicker and sicker. First week of August, I went in and talked to her. She said, "Honey, I'm not going to make it." I said, "Yeah, you are, Gladys."

I told Elvis, "If we don't get her out of here, she's going to die on us." She was starting to turn yellow. Her jaundice was there and the whole thing. But he wouldn't let her go, until I got in a big fight with him. I said, "You're just going to have to do it. She's going to die here on you if you don't get her back to Memphis." So he finally let her go, but it was a war zone before we got her out of there.

We put her on a train, her and Vernon. Put them on a train, because she wouldn't fly, and sent her back to Memphis from Temple, Texas. I said to Elvis, "Just get an emergency leave." So Elvis went to his company commander and got an emergency leave. We flew to Memphis from Fort Worth and went straight to the hospital. She died 48 hours later. It was that close.

Q. Were you surprised by Elvis' reaction when he found out his mom died?

A. He cried. He came apart. It happened at the house. I had taken some girls and some people home. I came back. Grandmother Presley met me at the door. She said, "Gladys has just died." So I rushed down to the hospital. I took Grandma with me. I came off the elevator. You could hear Elvis screaming and crying down the hall. Pretty bad. The day before I had gone and seen Gladys. We talked. She always cared for me and I cared for her. The next day, she — just, boom, it was over with that evening. It happened, I think, around … I think it happened probably eleven, twelve at night. It was pretty bad for him.

Q. Was Gladys' death the most intense emotional moment Elvis ever had?

A. I believe so. When his mother died, it was tough on him. Real tough on him. In fact, he never really got over it. He never had time to grieve for her, because we went straight to Germany. He took a long, long time to get over it. In fact, he never really ever got over it, because he was so close to her. It was a case of where, you know, she died and he had to go. He got orders to leave, went to the funeral, came back to the Army and went to Germany. So he never had time to grieve. It was just, you know, boom, boom, boom!

25

Q. Were there other times you saw him come apart?

A. Sure. But never to that same degree. Never, ever again. It just didn't happen. That was his mother. He never, ever came apart like that again. He was in the Army. He didn't like that. We had to go straight to Germany. He talked about her endlessly. There wasn't anything he could do about it. He was in the Army and he had to do it. He didn't have a choice.

Q. Did Elvis feel in any way responsible for his mother's death?

A. No. No, he did more than enough. It was a case that she just didn't take care of herself. She was always scared about Elvis and stuff like that. Gladys' side of the family was not a long-lived family. Elvis' genetics, I guess, came from her, because he died in his forties like she did. Her family was very short-lived. She just didn't take care of herself. She was worried about Elvis, because he was an only child. She stayed scared the whole time that Elvis was a star. He was away from her all the time, and she didn't like that.

Here's a woman that walked behind Elvis to school, you know, when he was a child. He was an only child, because his twin died at birth. And she never got over it. She was really nervous about him. She drank a little bit and stuff like that, but it was just she did not take good care of herself. She started getting sicker and sicker. She had liver problems. That's what eventually killed her. I think it was partly the short life expectancy of the family itself, from her side; I think the other part is she just gave up. But it rattled him pretty bad. In fact, it shook him to the core.

* * *

~ <u>A</u> <u>Forever</u> <u>Friendship</u> ~

- July, 1953: Elvis auditions for a Memphis gospel group but is rejected because he can't sing harmony.

- August, 1953: Elvis makes a private acetate recording of *My Happiness* and *That's When Your Heartaches Begin* at Memphis Recording Service owned by Sam Phillips; Phillips' secretary, Marion Keisker, secretly tapes the session, writing a memo that notes "Pressley: good ballad singer".

- May, 1954: Phillips invites Elvis to record; several sessions yield no results until July 5-6, when Elvis records stunning new versions of *That's All Right, Mama* and *Blue Moon of Kentucky* (released on Sun Records July 19, 1954).

- Summer, 1954: Elvis' performances at local parks, hospitals, restaurants and drug stores cause audience hysteria; Elvis tells Sam Phillips he wants to be released from Sun Records and sing only gospel music.

- October 2, 1954: Elvis appears at Nashville's *Grand Ole Opry*; afterwards, the stage manager advises him to quit the music business.

- October 16, 1954: Elvis sings nationwide on CBS Radio Network's *Louisiana Hayride* for the first of 50 appearances at $18 per show; by year's end Elvis has recorded *Milkcow Blues Boogie*; *You're a Heartbreaker*; *I'm Left, You're Right, She's Gone*; *Baby, Let's Play House*; *Mystery Train*; *I Forgot To Remember To Forget* for Sun Records and is named by Billboard as eighth-most promising country-western singer of 1954.

Q. When did you first meet Elvis?

A. In early 1954. Sam Phillips introduced me to him. Elvis was getting ready to do *Blue Moon of Kentucky* and *That's All Right* at that recording session. Sam took me over to the studio, and I met Elvis there. It was before he even had a record out. That's when I met him, before the session. I came in and out of the session when he was doing it. I came over and listened to part of it, then left, and came back.

Q. How did you link up with Sam Phillips and his studio?

A. I had just graduated from high school in '54. I wanted to be a disc jockey and just one thing led to another. I liked Sam. Sam used to teach me the board. Sam was an engineer at a radio station underneath the Hotel Peabody, WREC-AM. That's where I met Sam. He had recorded Junior Parker and these various blues people.

One day Sam said, "I'd like you to hear somebody." So he took me over to Sun Records over there on Union and said, "I want you to hear this." He played Elvis' demo for me and said, "I think he's going to be a good ballad singer." I said, "Well, great."

So then about two or three months after that, he called me and said, "You want to come down to a session? I'm doing a session with that guy I played for you named Elvis."

I said, "Okay. Fine." That's when I went down and met Elvis. It was in July, 1954.

Q. What went through your mind the first time you heard Elvis' demo?

A. I didn't know that much about stuff right then. He just had a real high voice. I didn't know what Sam saw. I didn't even know what Sam was looking for. But then after he did the session with *That's All Right* and *Blue Moon of Kentucky*, I knew there was something there. He was just entirely different. I had never heard anything like him.

Q. What were your first impressions of Elvis as a person?

A. Just a real quiet, laid-back guy. He seemed very nervous, which I guess I would have been too. He was just different looking. He didn't look like anybody I'd ever seen in my life. Just entirely different. He had sideburns, stuff like that. I'd never seen anything like him. I was talking to him about the way he did *Blue Moon of Kentucky*, and I said, "Man, you're, you know, you're different. I don't know what you got, but there is something there, and it's unbelievable." I told him, I said, "I don't know what you're going to be, but if people take you like you are, I guess you'll do something."

Q. The friendship continued to build?

A. We talked. We got to be friends over a period of time. After that, he'd see me, and we'd talk. Whenever he came into Memphis, he'd give me a call. We'd get together. We hung out together and stuff like that in '54. In '55, he was going back and forth, he did a lot of his television stuff and everything.

Q. When did you formally start working with him?

A. In 1957, I was a disc jockey at country station KEBE-AM in Jacksonville, Texas. I'd bluffed my way into that job. I told them I had experience as a deejay, which I hadn't, but I'd been coached by George Klein back in Memphis. I was able to do an aircheck and that got me the job. I used the name "Don Lamar" because it had a better rhythm to it than Lamar Fike.

One day I got mad at my boss and put an LP on the turntable and left and quit. I got back to my house in Waco. I called Elvis up. He was getting ready to start filming *Jailhouse Rock*.

I got hold of him in the hospital. He had just swallowed a cap off his tooth. I said, "I've quit the radio station." He said, "Why don't you come out here?" I said, "Well, fine. What am I going to do?" He said, "Just come out here, and we'll work something out."

So I got in my car and drove out there to the West Coast. He was staying at the Beverly Wilshire, and I started with him then. I worked in *Jailhouse Rock* with him.

Elvis and I were just friends who became closer friends. It was one of the situations of where, you know, he said, "I want you to stay here." And I did. I just did it.

Q. Where was Elvis living when you first met?

A. When I first met Elvis in 1954, he was living over at 2414 Lamar Avenue in Memphis. When I'd hang around him in '55-'56, he lived in a house at 1034 Audubon Drive, out past Park Avenue. I'd go out there and visit. He bought Graceland before he started *Jailhouse Rock*. When I moved in with him and his family in 1957, I moved in to Graceland.

Q. At that point, were you almost part of the family?

A. Yeah, it was the truth. Gladys was like my mother. My momma's dead now, but I was away from home then. I was 23 years old. Gladys just really took a liking to me. There was no other term. I was just real, real close to Gladys — very, very close to her. She's the only one that understood it when Elvis would get mad at somebody. It was only me around at the house. I was the only one living with him at the time in '57.

When something went wrong, I'd go to Gladys. I'd say, "What the hell is he doing? What's going on?" She said, "This is what he's doing. This is why he's doing it."

She always told me something I never forgot. She said, "Always remember when Elvis gets in a fight with you, it's from the mouth out." It was her favorite expression. And I didn't understand it. She said, "He doesn't mean it. It's not from the heart. It's from the mouth. It's not coming from his heart."

Q. Would Elvis apologize?

A. Elvis never apologized. Elvis never said "I'm sorry" in his life over five, six times. He never said "I'm sorry" or "thank you". It just wasn't one of his favorite expressions, "I'm sorry". I think it was a trait of Elvis. He would do it in other ways. He would go out and buy you a car instead of saying "I'm sorry". It's a hell of a way to say "I'm sorry", but he did it. That's the way he'd do it. He never took back a gift. Once he gave us a car, he didn't care what we did with it. Sell it or what. He could care less.

Q. Is it true one time he threw a dart and it stuck in your leg?

A. Yeah, he'd do stuff like that. He hit me with a pool stick one time. He slugged me one time. He didn't do that again, either. He got mad at me and just hit me. Hit me with a three-layer cake one time, went all over me, in Germany. I said, "I've put up with you for two years over here. I don't want no more of this. I get through with you, you'll look like Swiss cheese." Then he made up with me.

As quickly as it happened, it would go the opposite direction. He had a violent temper. I mean, violent. He had one of the most violent tempers I believe I've ever seen before or since. He could have been a killer, if he wanted to be. You'd know when he was there. Just certain ticks was the way he'd do it. He'd explode. I'd push him. A lot of times I'd push him there, but boy, his temper was scary. Scary temper.

Q. But even some of the temper episodes had a humorous side?

A. Once, we were riding motorcycles, and the road was slick. I slid under a bus and was pinned under it. They had to take a big wrecker to pull the bus off of me. When Elvis got real scared, he would laugh. I was up under the bus. People were gathering around him, he was signing autographs. I said, "I'm up under this bus. I might die. This thing might blow up." And he thought that was funny until they finally lifted the bus off of me. I couldn't get out from under it. He was on the concrete laughing. It was serious. And the madder I got at him, the more he'd laugh.

Q. Did the whole crew ride the motorcycles at night around town?

A. A lot of us did, yeah, not all. A lot of the guys wouldn't, but I would. Elvis and I would come down Highway 51 in Memphis, which is now called Elvis Presley Boulevard. We'd top the road, and we'd open them wide open to see how fast we could get. We would hold hands. He'd reach over and grab my hand, I'd grab his. And the throttle hands were still on the throttle. And we'd see who would turn chicken before we turned into the driveway. We were young, 23-24 years old. You never think you're going to die. I've turned in that driveway with my floorboards — where you put your feet was called the floorboards — just sparking. Barely made it into the driveway. It would just be that close.

Q. What do you remember as an instance of a real kindness he showed toward you?

A. I went into hospital for an operation, an intestinal bypass. He had a phone put in next to my bed and had the hospital switchboard leave the line open for the whole three days of the surgery and recovery. He would just pick up the phone and start talking. "Are you okay?" My cousin Tommy McDonald was there and he'd say, "Lamar's fine, Elvis. He's okay. He just came out of surgery." He asked Tommy for updates about every couple hours, checking on me literally around the clock. He cared, and he showed it.

Q. Did you always know what Elvis was thinking?

A. Oh, yeah. I always knew what he thought. Elvis and I would be sitting in a room. Something would happen. He'd look at me. I'd look at him. We'd just get up and leave. We were already talking to each other. We were like brothers. Brothers are that way. Twins are that way. We were that way. We knew what each other was thinking. We had to around him, because it was hard enough following him as it was. Elvis was like — it was like following a ping-pong ball. You didn't know where he was going to bounce. But you had to try to figure it out.

Q. How would Elvis show his displeasure with you guys?

A. Elvis just didn't talk. He would walk away. He would shut down. The clue with Elvis was when he shut down. When he didn't talk, you knew something was wrong.

Q. Were you ever fired?

A. I was fired about 300 times. Maybe 400. And then he'd hire me back. Everybody got fired. He just did it. He fired me more than anybody, because I was always arguing with him.

Q. Were you one of the few who would actually confront him?

A. I would confront him. I'd say, "Hey, that's enough of that. I'll see you later." I'd leave and go down the hill. He'd call about an hour later and say to come back. I'd say, "It's okay, but I'm not going to put up with it."

Q. Was there anything that you ever held back from him?

A. No. He'd come off from doing a show in Vegas or something. The guys said Elvis was good. Each guy would say, "That was a good show." We'd all be sitting there and everything. He'd just walk right by me. I said, "You gonna ask me?" He said, "No, I'm not." And he'd go in the bedroom.

Then he'd go back in the dressing room and call me and say, "What did you think?" I'd say, "Piece of shit. Worst show I've ever seen in my life."

He said, "I knew I didn't want to hear it." I said, "Well, don't ask." And he wouldn't ask me unless he wanted to hear it.

I'm that way today. If I don't like something, you just heard me. I don't pull back. I have no compunctions about that. Elvis used to tell them, "If you don't want to find out an answer to a question, don't ask Lamar. Just don't ask him. Leave him alone."

Q. Did Elvis have to mediate disputes among his inner circle?

A. Elvis called one of the guys in one time and said, "I want to explain something to you." He said, "In my life, I have things that I have to do and things that I have to put up with." And he said, "Lamar Fike answers to me. He don't answer to anybody else. It's rough enough having Lamar with me, but I sure as hell don't need y'all to aggravate him. Because when you do, he makes my life miserable, and then I make y'all's life miserable."

He said, "When he makes my life miserable, y'all are nothing but problems. So leave him alone. Don't tell him what to do. You ask him. Then if he feels like doing it, he will. And if he won't, he'll just walk off from you."

And that's the way I am.

If Elvis would ask me to do something, I'd go do it. Every once in a while, he'd tell me, and I'd do it. But he said, "Nobody tells Lamar in this group what to do but me. That's the way it's going to be. And that's the way it'll be until he dies, or as long as he is with me."

So that's the way it was with him. I wasn't different. That's just the way I was. I was with him.

Q. Did Colonel want you to be the spy inside Elvis' camp?

A. I wouldn't. Also, I didn't like Colonel ordering me around. I said, "Just leave me alone." I mean, I was 40 years old then. I didn't want to put up with that.

Q. Did Elvis demand total loyalty from his employees and friends?

A. Elvis extracted outright loyalty. He either got it, or you weren't there. So we were all real loyal to him. I never did a book about Elvis when he was alive. I only spoke out after he was dead. My loyalty toward a person who is not here anymore is over with. When they die, that drops the law.

Q. Aside from yourself, who would you say was Elvis' closest confidant, the person to whom he would tell his deepest thoughts?

A. His cousin Billy Smith, the last part of his life, was his closest friend. Billy was like a son almost, or little brother. He raised Billy, and they were real close. My thing with Elvis was, there was a lot of adversarial stuff, but we were real close. The latter part of the years, I was out with the Colonel. I'd go out ahead, because I couldn't put up with Elvis. He'd drive me crazy.

So I'd go out with the Colonel in the tour advance so as not to be around Elvis all the time, because he was just ... to keep from him and I getting in each other's throat or me getting fired, I told him I'd go out with the Colonel. "I'll set up the hotels for you and everything." That's why I was in Portland, Maine, when he died. I was setting up his hotel for the tour.

Q. Over the years since his death, have you ever had moments where you experience his presence physically? As if he were in the room with you?

A. Absolutely. There's not a night goes by I don't dream about him. He's in my dreams. He'll walk through my dreams. Somewhere, he'll walk through. I dream about him every night of my life. I still do. I have no reason to. I'm sitting here talking. But you know, I mean, every day, there is something on Elvis every day of my life. It's just, he talks to me. I've had him wake me up in the middle of night screaming my name out. I've stood up straight in the middle of bed. Used to scare my ex-wife to death.

Q. Do you actually hear his voice?

A. He screams at me, "Lamar, wake up!"

Q. Do you think he saw you as a brother he never had?

A. I don't know. He used to laugh about it. We had dark hair. I had dark circles under my eyes like he did. A lot of stuff came about. Even when I was not around Elvis, he was calling, checking on me and stuff like that. We were pretty close. Real close. But it's just like I told Elvis, it's second billing. I'll be a second banana until the day I die, but that's okay. It's just part of it. And I don't mind that. I don't.

It was difficult at times having to spend the time with Elvis, but that was my choice. We all make choices throughout our life, and that was one of mine. There are consequences, and these can be good and bad.

Q. Do you think the two of you were fated to be friends?

A. It could be. I don't know. It was one of those things where we were together so long. I think it's just fate, I guess. I don't know if it was meant to be or whatever. I guess this was being at the right place at the right time. Everybody wants to make something out of their life, I guess. Nobody thinks that they are historic. But now, history is where I'm set. I had the privilege to share the life of one of the biggest superstars the world has ever known.

* * *

~ **Elvis** **Meets** **America**: **The** **1950s** ~

- "He is the most obscene, vulgar influence on America today … I consider him a menace to young girls."
  — *Hedda Hopper, newspaper columnist*

- "Elvis is a real decent, fine boy." — *Ed Sullivan, TV host*

- "I wouldn't let my daughter walk across the street to see Elvis Presley perform." — *Rev. Billy Graham*

- "I don't feel I'm doin' anything wrong." — *Elvis Presley*

THE MUSIC AND performance style of Elvis Presley defined a decade. More than the Eisenhower Era, the American 1950s were truly the Elvis Era, as the "Hillbilly Cat" from Mississippi became the literal poster boy for pop music's emerging rock 'n' roll idiom.

Though earlier singers had sparked enthusiastic fan response, the adulation (and virulence) directed at Elvis was entirely new in its range and intensity. Your opinion about Elvis was more than a matter of musical preference; it spoke volumes about who you were in terms of age, personality, political orientation and social class.

By the end of the 1950s, Elvis Presley was not only the most recognized name in the world but an unintentional catalyst for social change. The critics were right: Elvis and his music really did make young people go crazy … and there were plenty of folks, especially in the entertainment industry, who thought that was a Very Good Thing.

Q. In the beginning, was Elvis insecure about the mass media recognition?

A. It got pretty busy, yeah. That's when he started laying back. He didn't go out as much. It got worse and worse.

Q. Did he feel concerned about going out in public?

A. No, he could go out. He'd ride his motorcycle around. But he'd pull a crowd together pretty fast. There was a time in Memphis in '57 where Elvis and me and a couple of the guys would go to movies all day long. We'd go to two or three shows in a day, and nobody would bother us that much. They would crowd around us, but we'd actually just pay and go into the movies. We'd see movies two or three hours a day. We didn't have anything to do, so we'd go downtown. We'd go to one movie, come out and go into another one. It was just fun.

Q. Early in his career, when Elvis was called "the Hillbilly Cat", did he take that as a slur?

A. That wasn't a slur. They were trying to figure out a way to cross him from country into pop into R&B or whatever it was back then. It was not rock 'n' roll yet. They didn't know what it was. His music was called rockabilly back then.

Q. What about Elvis' appearance, clothes and sideburns?

A. He liked the way the black people dressed. He loved that. He thought that was the slickest way to dress. He wore a lot of black, pink, bright colors. Nobody else white dressed like that. The sideburns he liked because truck drivers wore them. He thought that was neat. Long-haul truck drivers had long sideburns. That was their label. It's called pork chops.

Q. Before he became famous, was he confronted about his appearance?

A. The guys would make fun of him, the way he dressed, yeah. And he'd just blow them off. He would do it out of necessity, because he never fit in. Elvis didn't fit in with anybody. He was a loner. He was different.

Q. Was he bitter about the *Grand Ole Opry* rejection?

A. We went to the Opry in October, 1954. They didn't like it because he had drums, and he was too rock 'n' roll for them. Elvis never forgot. He didn't like being embarrassed at the Opry. Didn't like it at all. Didn't like anything about the Opry. He never forgot.

Q. Did you and Elvis tour Canada?

A. We did two tours of Canada in '56 and '57. Just didn't work out. He never went back again. He was very successful. In '57 he played against the Canadian Exposition in Montreal and outdrew it. Their attendance dropped down to like 90% of normal because Elvis was in town and everyone knew it. We played a football field close to it and outdrew them.

The fact of the matter was, that was the last tour until 1969. The second Canada tour was just too much. Crowds, bad sound systems, transportation hassles. It soured all of us for many years on touring. Elvis started doing movies, then went into the Army, and we didn't do any more tours for the next dozen years.

Q. Did being perceived as an exponent of "devil's music" bother him?

A. No, not really. Elvis never worried about that. He knew he wasn't a devil, so he never worried about it. He just said, "I don't understand why they're doing it." He said, "I think it's ridiculous."

I said, "Well, it's all part of it." He said, "What am I doing wrong?"

I said, "Nothing I know of. Just keep doing what you're doing." I said, "Hell, if they don't like it, they're going to tell you." And I said, "If they don't like it, then your career will be over with, and they didn't like you in the first place."

Well, that never happened. He caused young people to wake up. Before Elvis, popular music was Sinatra and Dean Martin and all these people. Elvis was a young guy that came in and really pioneered it. I mean, here's a guy 19 years old had a monster hit.

He was selling records 90 miles a minute. He changed the face of rock 'n' roll. He really literally put rock 'n' roll on the map. He brought the youth into it, and that's what never had been.

Q. In the 1950s, did Elvis see himself as a leader of a social movement?

In the 1950s, American kids had no leader. They had nobody to identify with. There was no identity in rock 'n' roll back then — we didn't even call it rock 'n' roll. It was a generation of just really zero, there was nothing there that anybody could cling onto. We're talking a generation that when the hem line went up, panic set in. It was a very conservative generation. And they damned rock 'n' roll because it just tore people's heads up.

As one person, what he did was he literally kick the door open for his generation. And he didn't do it on purpose, it just happened. When he kicked the door open, it just, my God man, it was like somebody opened a floodgate! Behind him came everything. He literally grabbed the young generation and the entertainment industry by the damned shirt and drug them through.

I loved Jackie Gleason, but back then Jackie's great statement on Elvis was, "This kid will never make it. This kid can't last." Elvis emerging onto the scene rattled everybody in entertainment. In religion, politics, business, fashion, everything.

Always remember one thing, nobody likes change. The most insecure a person will ever get in their life is when they have to change their routines. But in order to stay on the edge, you have to change your routine everyday, and he was changing their routine whether they liked it or not. They had to address the situation, they couldn't ignore it.

Q. His social importance transcended his importance as a performer?

A. He became an iconic Standard. Once I was talking to a photographer at MGM. I said what do you use as a standard? He said, "A standard in our business is Elizabeth Taylor. Anything that deviates up or down from her is the comparison factor."

The analogy in the music business is Elvis. Anything new that has come along, any style, any performer, band or whatnot, the media use Elvis as a comparison factor — records sales, concerts, public reactions, societal impact. He became a Standard of our time determining what somebody is or isn't going to be.

Q. What was the first rush of celebrity like for Elvis?

A. It was frantic there the first three years. It was real frantic. No preparation for it. It was just, boom! It was just, "Here we go!" All of '57 was like a madhouse.

Dewey Phillips broke the record, the first record, *That's Alright, Mama*, on his *Red, Hot and Blue* radio show. He basically just kept it on a constant rotation for hours. All day long. Back then you could do it. Elvis was at Suzore No. 2 Theatre on Main Street. He was up in the balcony with his date. Somebody came and got him and said, "Listen, man. They're playing the shit out of that record. They want you to come down to WHBQ." And that's where Elvis went down there and did his first media interview on the air live with Dewey.

The media, the newspapers and the magazines in Memphis started getting on it, yeah. You had a hometown boy making good. Then Sam signed, you know, the rest of the guys, Carl Perkins and Johnny Cash.

I was with Elvis one day and we met Johnny Cash on the street. He asked the direction to Sun Records. He worked on refrigerators, air conditioners, stuff like that. We were down at Ace Appliance Company. That's where Cash worked.

At first Elvis was very regional — Texas, Louisiana, parts of Tennessee, Mississippi. He was a very regional act. What broke Elvis out was RCA. When he sold his contract to RCA, that's what broke Elvis big. Colonel put him with RCA and then put the publishing deals together with Jean and Julian Aberbach at Hill & Range Publishing and their subsidiary, Elvis Presley Music, operated by the Aberbachs' cousin, Freddie Bienstock.

Elvis' first records were 78 rpms. 45s weren't widespread through the South until the late '50s. It was all regional back then. Elvis didn't get nationwide and worldwide until his RCA records started coming out in 1956. That's when it all broke out. Nobody had heard of Elvis outside of maybe seven or eight states, Southern states below the Mason Dixon Line. When Elvis went to RCA, then everybody heard him.

Q. Was Elvis' early success aided by radio payola?

A. Well, I'm quite sure there was some of that, but I mean, who knew it? I didn't. We didn't. Elvis was never at that level. Elvis never knew what it took to get a record from where it was to where it is. He didn't know that. He didn't know about copyrights. Elvis didn't even know what the word copyright meant. He didn't know. Although he owned two big publishing companies, he didn't know.

Q. You're saying Elvis was completely distanced from his business affairs?

A. Elvis did not want to know anything but what he did, which was to perform, and that's what he knew, and he didn't care about anything else. He did not care about the mechanics of things. He did not like the mechanics of stuff. Broke? Fix it. Get it out of here. If you can't fix it, buy another one. That's the only thing he knew. Go on, get it fixed, buy it, go buy something else.

Q. What happened when Elvis fired his first band?

A. It was the Colonel who fired the band. That happened in 1957 before we did the Tupelo Fair. They felt like they deserved more than what Elvis was giving them. The Colonel said, "You don't deserve anymore than that." So he fired them.

Elvis said, "What are we going to do?" Colonel said, "We'll get another band."

And we did. After that, there were no more problems. We got the best musicians you could get.

In the early days, one of the band members, Scotty Moore, was actually managing the money before the Colonel came on. Scotty had a contract with Elvis. Scotty and Bill were all pissed off at the Colonel and wanted a bigger share of the pie. The Colonel said, "That's not going to happen."

Q. Was there any tension between Elvis and the original band members when they appeared on the *'68 Comeback Special*?

A. No. The boys were just glad to do the show. After the *Comeback Special*, there never were any tensions. D.J. Fontana would be around, because Elvis liked D.J. and put him on the some of the sessions. I mean, Elvis didn't associate D.J. with Scotty and Bill because when they quit, when they threatened to quit, D.J. just said to Elvis, "I'm with you, chief." That's what D.J. said. "I'm with you. I play drums. That's the end of it."

Scotty and Bill got in this whole big thing, you know, and that's what broke the whole deal up. But then there came a time when D.J. wasn't around anymore. When we'd get away from somebody, they never came back. He just sort of drifted away from them.

Q. The audience in the early days, was it predominantly women or was it mixed?

A. It was mixed. The latter part of Elvis' career, it became a family show. Like I told him, "Elvis, you've turned into the Walt Disney of rock 'n' roll. All the families come." Rock 'n' roll got so raunchy by the mid-'70s that Elvis was the only family-oriented show working. Look at the stuff going on out there by then. My God, Elvis was the cleanest act out there.

Q. Did Elvis complain about being made to sing to the hound dog on the Steve Allen Show?

A. He never forgave Steve Allen for it. He felt like they made a fool of him. Elvis didn't forget. He liked Milton Berle, he always liked Milton. But Steve he never cared for. Never forgave him at all.

Q. What did Elvis think of Ed Sullivan?

A. He liked Ed Sullivan. One of his last Ed Sullivan appearances, he sang *Peace in the Valley*, gospel. Ed was genuinely impressed and came out on stage and said what a good person Elvis was. Elvis never saw him again after that.

* * *

~ **Elvis and the Colonel** ~

ELVIS' MANAGER, Colonel Tom Parker (1909-97), has been called a master promoter, a merchandising genius, a visionary architect of the modern music industry — and one of the worst manipulators and abusers of talent in history.

One thing is certain: within a year after taking over full management of Elvis in November, 1955, Parker's business savvy (and good timing) had established his client as the richest and best-known music star in the world.

A former carnival show operator and manager of country music acts, Parker claimed to be a native of Huntington, West Virginia. In the 1980s, it was revealed he had, in fact, been born Andreas van Kujik in Breda, Netherlands, had jumped a merchant marine ship in 1929 and entered the U.S. illegally, possibly as a fugitive from committing a murder overseas.

Parker's gambling addiction and losses grew worse in the late 1960s and are believed to be the reason he negotiated several contracts that were detrimental to Elvis' financial, physical and mental health.

Q. Where did the Colonel first see Elvis?

A. Colonel first saw him on the *Louisiana Hayride* show in early 1955. The *Louisiana Hayride* wasn't like the *Grand Ole Opry* in Nashville. It was different, less exclusive. Everybody was on the show. My God, everybody was there. That's where Colonel first saw him. That's where it all transpired from.

Q. Was Elvis interested in signing with the Colonel right away?

A. No, he didn't know anything about him. Sam Phillips said there were two people he'd let manage Elvis. Elvis said, "Who's that?" Sam said, "It'd be my brother Jud or else Colonel Parker." And thank God he didn't get Jud, you know. He got Colonel Parker, and that's the way it all came about.

Colonel was nice to Gladys and real nice to Vernon. You know, Vernon said something to Colonel one time. I was there when it happened. He told Colonel, he said, "Colonel, I'm the one that got Elvis on the *Louisiana Hayride*." Colonel said, "I did one better. I got him off."

Q. Did Elvis ever express to you serious resentment about the Colonel?

A. At the end, yeah. He didn't like him. They got in big fights. Colonel's gambling got the best of him. Elvis didn't like it. He felt like he was trapped in Vegas. He didn't like Las Vegas. He hated Las Vegas. At the end, the last couple of years of his life, he detested it, but Colonel had signed these enormous, long-term contracts. Elvis was doing Vegas two, three, four times a year. That's a lot. Four weeks at a whack. That's a long time. Nobody does that anymore. Nobody's alive that's doing that. Colonel had Elvis doing two shows a day. Sometimes three. And it wore him out.

I think Vegas had more to do with Elvis' death than anything. It caused him a lot of problems. He was just working. The Colonel had gambled so much that Elvis felt like he was paying his bills, and he didn't like it. At the end, before Elvis died, their relationship was really thin.

Q. Was the Colonel's citizenship problem the reason he never allowed Elvis to perform outside the continental United States?

A. The Colonel was an alien, literally. He jumped ship. He was supposed to have killed somebody in Holland, in Breda, where he lived as a young man. I went to Breda and met his sister and everybody else.

But the Colonel died here. He never went out of the continental United States. He went into Canada, but he didn't go anywhere else that required a passport. He stayed within the continental boundaries of North America.

Q. Is it truth or myth that Colonel was not such a vigilant business person?

A. He was shrewd, but he wasn't a good businessman at all. He spent awfully fast. His big spending was gambling. He was a gambling junkie. I mean, he was as bad with gambling as Elvis was with drugs. One of the big fights that Colonel and I had, I used to tell him, "You can't sit here and accuse Elvis of being what he is and you being what you are." He said, "What are you saying?"

I said, "You're a damn gambling junkie." He used to get mad at me about it. "Well, it's none of your business." I said, "Everybody in the hotel sees you doing it."

I was sitting there at a craps table one night. I was up a quarter million dollars, and he came up and took the whole quarter million, shoved it on the line against 'don't pass', and I lost a quarter million in one roll. I got sick.

I told him, I said, "That's a lot of money!" "Well, I'll give it back to you." I never got it back.

Q. Did the Colonel ever influence what songs Elvis sang?

A. Tried to. Colonel suggested one song that was a hit that Elvis didn't know. It was called *Are You Lonesome Tonight?* Colonel liked it by Blue Barron. He always thought that was great. Blue Barron had it out first. Blue Barron and his orchestra. Colonel always liked the song, and he got Elvis to do it. Elvis didn't want to do it. He said, "Well, I'll just do it." Then Elvis ended up loving the song.

Q. Was the agreement between Elvis and the Colonel a handshake deal?

A. No, it was a contract. Never a handshake. Never, ever. That's a myth, absolutely. The big problems they had the last year-and-a-half, two years of Elvis' life was that, because the Colonel wanted to renew the contracts, and Elvis didn't want the Colonel anymore. He was going to get rid of him.

Q. Is it true the Colonel got 50% of all Elvis' income?

A. That's what they say. But back then, a lot of artists had 50/50 deals with their managers. It was no big deal back then. I mean, now, of course, it is. I don't think it was a good contract at all. And I think in the last couple of years of Elvis' life — I'd say the last four or five years of his life — he started resenting all that.

But Elvis, just like I said, he would not confront the Colonel. He would send messages back and forth to the Colonel either with me or with Joe Esposito, and they'd get me in the middle of the argument, but Elvis wouldn't confront him. Finally, he confronted him up there one day, and they got in a big screaming fight, but I don't know what happened. After that, I think he just finally went ahead and re-signed.

Q. Elvis was really going to get rid of the Colonel as his manager?

A. He was going to get rid of the Colonel. Yeah, the Colonel was on his way out. But Elvis didn't trust anybody. It goes back to that original thing. He didn't trust anybody else. He didn't want anybody coming in from the outside telling him what to do. Colonel knew that. Colonel was a great student of human nature. If Colonel couldn't do anything else, he knew human nature. And Elvis did not trust anybody else, so Colonel played on that.

As a consequence, Elvis wouldn't get an outside manager, because he didn't want anybody to know his business. So he stayed with the Colonel, even though it was uncomfortable.

Elvis didn't like to change things. He did not like change. He didn't want it. Didn't like it. In fact, out on the road, we'd land in different places. His bathroom was set up just like it was at Graceland. It was never changed. IIis bathroom was always the same. They set up his bathroom a certain way. He could go in there in the dark and reach for the toothpaste and know where it was. He didn't like change. He would have never had another manager, because he didn't trust them.

Q. Were there decisions the Colonel made that harmed Elvis?

A. Sure. The biggest harm was that he signed that contract we did in Vegas. Four weeks at a pop. Good God. The Colonel gambled so much that Elvis was paying his gambling bills. The Colonel was just an inveterate gambler. Worst I've ever seen. The Colonel was a carnie man. He was raised in a carnival. That's what he based all his life on.

The Colonel lived pretty elaborately in his own way. I mean, at the Hilton Hotel, he had the whole wing of the hotel. He had 20-some-odd rooms all the way down to the end of the hall and had his bed set up in one, a cook house in it, and the whole thing. Colonel lived very lavishly when he was in Vegas.

Colonel influenced Elvis in more ways than one. Like he wouldn't take any outside deals to make money. The Colonel would discourage that. Elvis never endorsed anything. The only commercial he ever did was one time in Killeen, Texas. He endorsed a trailer. Right before Colonel had him, he endorsed donuts, a donut company in Memphis. He did a jingle called *You Get Them Piping Hot After 4 P.M.* But Elvis never endorsed anything — never, ever. God, the money he could have made at that!

Merchandising was different. They had teddy bears and stuff like that. From the very beginning the Colonel did merchandising. The whole United States and everywhere else. Merchandising was the Colonel's game. He was a carnie. He knew how to do that.

Q. Did the Colonel try to influence how Elvis spent or invested his money?

A. The Colonel never influenced or advised Elvis what to do with his money. He would stay out of it. Elvis would always pay every cent of his taxes on his own.

Q. Did Elvis and the Colonel have daily contact?

A. They talked to each other every day but weren't around each other that much. Colonel's assistant, Tom Diskin, would come by with contracts from the Colonel. Elvis would sign them. Never even read them. Signed them. If we were on the film set or something, Colonel would see him every day.

As a rule, Colonel had his group of guys around him, and Elvis had his group. We were two different groups. We were never in the same camp. Colonel didn't hang around Elvis. Elvis didn't hang around the Colonel. The group would. Some of the guys would. He'd have his guys to keep contact to give him information on what was going on inside. Because if not, he wouldn't have got any information, because our guys wouldn't tell him.

Q. Was this internal espionage common knowledge among you all?

A. Yeah, everybody in the group knew it. Tried to tell Elvis. He wouldn't listen.

Q. Did the Colonel elevate himself to the same level as Elvis?

A. He tried to. When different stars would open, Colonel would send out 100 telegrams saying, "Congratulations on the opening, Elvis and the Colonel." It was "Elvis and the Colonel", always, "Elvis and the Colonel". That's the way he established his name.

The ego was a massive ego. Enormous. They clashed a lot on account of that. He had his group of guys around him just like we did. He had four or five guys around him all the time, just like Elvis did.

Q. Elvis' name often appeared as co-writer on his early songs. Did the Colonel insist on that when negotiating for the song?

A. Elvis got a third of the writer's share. Elvis was so strong at the beginning that he would get a third of the song, but Elvis never knew he did. He'd get all of the publishing. It's just something he never paid any attention to. It'd be on there. He didn't understand why. He never checked it. Like I said, he never changed. This was something he didn't want to know. He didn't know anything about business. Could care less about it. He let Colonel take care of that, and he took care of the other stuff, putting on the show. He never knew what he was into, what he was doing, how it was going on, or what the deals were on the contracts. He just signed them.

The Colonel set it up, and it was that way. But toward the end, he couldn't command that. He couldn't do it anymore, but he used to do it at the beginning. That was the publishing company set up with Colonel Parker and Jean and Julian Aberbach. It was Elvis Presley Music and Gladys Music. One was ASCAP, one was BMI. That was for albums and for the movies, everything. Later on, it changed, because he wasn't selling like he was before.

Colonel could make any kind of deal he wanted to, because he had a complete situation. Elvis agreed with everything. So when you dealt with Elvis, you dealt with the Colonel. You didn't deal with Elvis. That's where the problem was.

Colonel controlled everything. Colonel controlled Elvis. He was literally the person. You could not do anything. If you asked Elvis about a deal, he'd say, "Go talk to the Colonel." He never would answer. He'd never say, "Let me hear your deal." He never would. He'd say, "Talk to the Colonel."

We were instructed never to talk business with anybody. Have them talk to the Colonel. That was drilled into us, and it was drilled into Elvis. A deal came, a guy came up with a deal, Elvis said, "Go talk to the Colonel. I don't do that." He would deflect them immediately.

And then Elvis got mad about the movie scripts later on. He said, "I don't want to do these scripts anymore." I said, "Well, Elvis, you've got to start taking control."

He said, "Colonel signed already." I said, "You signed them, too, Elvis."

Q. After the early years, Elvis wasn't on TV that much. Was that a strategy of the Colonel?

A. That was Colonel's design. Didn't put him much out there. Just put him in movies. Colonel always believed if you were on TV a lot, they wouldn't come see you. So he kept him out of it. He kept him out of the public eye a lot on purpose. Colonel helped create that mystique.

Q. So there was never a move to give Elvis his own TV variety show like Dean Martin or Sonny and Cher?

A. He never would have done it. Elvis wouldn't even do *The Tonight Show*. He couldn't talk to anybody. What's he going to tell you? Elvis didn't know how to talk to them. He wouldn't know what to do. That Sinatra show he did, with Sinatra singing his songs and Elvis singing Sinatra's. It was just that one instance they did. We did that after we came back from Germany. We had a private railroad car. Went down there. They put us in the Railroad Yards there in Miami. He went in to sing. It was Sinatra's idea. Elvis said, "Let's try it."

So they did. Came out pretty good. Sinatra couldn't pay Elvis. He didn't know what to do. Didn't have enough money.

Colonel said, "Listen, here's the way we do it." He put it on closed circuit inside the hotel and got the hotel to put up an extra $100,000 to pay Elvis.

Q. Was the Colonel a nice person, or was he just a tyrant?

A. Colonel was a nice person, but everybody was a mark to him. He grew up in the carnival. To carnies, you know, everybody is a mark. He had to know what was going on with his act. Any manager wants to know what his act is doing.

Q. Did the Colonel ever express any intentions of picking up another artist besides Elvis?

A. No, that's all he did. He had Elvis. Look, every manager in the world wants what happened to Colonel to happen to them. It happened to a guy here in Nashville with Garth Brooks. You get an artist like that, you don't need any other artist. Who the hell else you need? Have a guy making $150 million a year. You want to go out and get another act and spend time with him? You don't need it.

You get one act, he's making the money that Elvis made … I mean, they said the most Elvis ever made in one year was about $20-25 million. Well, that was 1965-70 money. Today, that's equal to what, $150-200 million? So why do you need another artist?

Q. Were your salaries always paid in cash?

A. No, it was checks. We'd pick up the checks every Friday at Graceland. I never missed a check in the whole time I was with Elvis — never, ever. Nobody ever did. Elvis never liked to sign checks. Vernon would sign the checks. There was a cabinet right when you go down the steps, the back steps going into the living room from Elvis' bedroom, back servant steps. That's where Elvis went up and down.

You'd come right down those steps. Right to the right was a little cabinet there, a little hanging cabinet, and there was a round thing on the corner there, and all the checks were put in there. They were signed by Vernon. $365 a week is the highest I ever made.

Q. Did you have a good rapport with the Colonel?

A. I did at the beginning. At the end, we fought all the time. I talked to Colonel about six months before he died. Freddie Bienstock arranged it where we would call each other without calling each other. We talked on the phone. We talked about 20 minutes on the phone.

Q. What was the outcome?

A. Nothing. He didn't need anything I had. I didn't need anything he had.

* * *

~ **Elvis** **and** **Uncle** **Sam** ~

- March 24, 1958: Elvis Presley is inducted into the U.S. Army; fans despair, but he continues to record and moves his mother and father to a house in Killeen, Texas, near his post at Fort Hood.

- August 14, 1958: Gladys Presley dies; October 1, Elvis arrives in West Germany to serve with the Seventh Army in Bad Nauheim.

- December, 1958: Elvis passes Bing Crosby as the most successful recording artist of all time as Colonel Parker maintains a steady campaign of record releases and publicity spots.

- March 23, 1960: Elvis arrives back in the U.S., honorably discharged from the Army as a sergeant; three nights later he gives a television performance on *The Frank Sinatra-Timex Special* for $125,000; Elvis' first stereo LP, *Elvis Is Back*, is released April 3 and hits $1 million in sales in three weeks.

Q. What was Elvis' first reaction to getting drafted into the Army?

A. It was around Christmas time, and we were at Graceland, talking, you know. He showed me the letter and said, "Boy, how about this shit?" I said, "You are going to go from $200,000 a month to $78. It's going to be a hell of a come down."

Q. Did he worry being away two years would end his career?

A. It scared him to death. He thought his career was going to be over with. Going into service has killed a lot of careers. It killed Eddie Fisher's career. Elvis thought he'd be out of sight that long and not recording, that it was going to be over with. I mean, he was worried sick, worried the whole time. That's why we would go out different places in Paris and stuff like that to let them see him. He knew what he was doing.

Elvis didn't like being away from that attention. We went to Paris, and boy, we tore that town apart, but he liked it, because he was able to get out there amongst them, and that was all part of the strategy of himself. No, he didn't like the Army. He didn't like anything about it.

Q. Did the Colonel try and get him out?

A. No, never did. He accepted it. Didn't like it but accepted it.

Q. Do you think maybe the government intentionally tried to take Elvis "out of circulation"?

A. There's always those kind of theories. No, I don't think that's true. Not at all. No. Why would you want to cut somebody up that's paying more taxes than anybody in the country? I think his number came up, and they hit him, you know. Back then, the draft was still ongoing. I got drafted the same year. I didn't think it was a conspiracy on me. Hey, the Army didn't want the problem of his celebrity. I mean, when he hit them, we scared them to death.

Q. Did Elvis get a temporary delay of induction?

A. Elvis had to finish up *King Creole*. He got a deferment for three months to finish that up. After he finished *King Creole* is when he went in.

Q. How did you end up going with him to Germany?

A. I tried to enlist, but my weight at the time exceeded the guidelines. He went to Fort Hood for basic training. When he came back from Fort Hood, he was on leave. He talked to me. He said, "I've got to go back to Fort Hood. Then I've got to go to Germany. Would you go?" I said, "Yeah, I'll go. Sure. No problem."

And so I packed up and got my shots and the whole thing, and off I went. We went back to Fort Hood. I stayed at a motel in Killeen,

Texas, until we rented the Mayor's house. I would drive on the base every day in a Lincoln convertible. The MPs would stop me every 20 feet, just harassing me and stuff like that.

Q. Why did they harass you?

A. I'm picking up a private in the Army in what was back then, a $10,000 convertible. The highest money you paid for a car was $2,200. They didn't like it. They didn't like it at all.

Q. Did the Army have a "hands-off" policy on Elvis?

A. People didn't really tell him what to do in the Army. They left Elvis alone. He was a big problem. Eisenhower put a cloak of secrecy around Elvis the whole time he was in. The president instructed the CIA and everybody else to leave him alone — "Don't let anybody know what he's doing." We had a cloak of secrecy around us for the whole 18 months we were in Europe.

Could have been a lot of reasons. It was bad enough to have Elvis Presley in the Army. He was more well-known than the president! They didn't want any problems. Elvis was treated with respect. He did things like a regular soldier and everything like that, but they didn't mess with him too often. They left him alone.

Q. What happened when Elvis arrived in Germany?

A. He got off that boat in Bremerhaven, and boy, I mean it's like the end of the world. They didn't know whether to shit or go blind. They had to literally, you know, surround him to get him off. And then he got to the camp. They said he will have to serve guard duty like everybody else; we said fine. They put him out there on guard duty one night in that little round thing, you know, and it took 30 men to get him out because of the crowds.

Q. Did Elvis have to try hard to conceal his frustration with the military?

A. He was unhappy with the Army because he didn't want to be in the Army. He didn't like it. He made the best out of a bad situation.

Q. Did he perform as part of any USO shows?

A. No. I remember when he turned Bob Hope down. Hope sent people up to where Elvis was on maneuver, and Elvis just said no, can't do it. It was cold, and he was into snow up to his ass, too. And he said you know, Lamar, I can get away from this thing and do it, and I said yeah, but I said, look at the problems. He didn't do it. Those guys came in and offered him a deal, and he said, nope. He didn't do it and went back to the barracks. That took guts.

Q. Was Elvis surprised at the reception he got when he returned to the States?

A. When we came back, we got on the train at Fort Dix, New Jersey. Colonel met us at Fort Dix. We had a private railroad car that belonged to the president of the railroad. They hooked our railroad car onto the end of it. We had a porter and a cook on the thing with us. Had three bedrooms. It had a big living room, dining room in it, the whole thing. Beautiful, private coach.

Everywhere we went, Colonel let the word out that Elvis was on that train, and the crowds were enormous every town we stopped. The back of the train had a porch or a veranda on the back of the private car, and Elvis would go out there and wave and sign autographs and talk at each city where it stopped. We never had to get off the car, because it was a private car. They just hooked it and moved it to another train if we had to change trains.

The Colonel had a picture for him to do right when we got back. I mean, boom! He was ready. Elvis went back straight into movies, even before we went back to the States. We started work on *GI Blues* before he got out of the Army.

They were doing second unit work in Germany when he was in his last five months of the Army. The producer Hal Wallis even came over. I met Mr. Wallis in Frankfurt. So he went straight into a picture right after he got out. Boom! He was working on the sound track, boom! It was just like that. He did the Sinatra television show in Miami and then went to Hollywood straight into finishing *GI Blues*.

* * *

~ <u>Elvis</u> <u>in</u> <u>Hollywood</u> ~

- From 1956-1969 Elvis Presley starred in 31 feature films, mostly musicals, that helped shift his image from a rebellious Elvis the Pelvis to an easygoing, guy-next-door persona.

- Elvis shared the screen with dozens of up-and-coming actresses (Ann-Margret, Raquel Welch, Nancy Sinatra, Mary Tyler Moore, Carolyn Jones, Shelley Fabares, Juliet Prowse, Debra Paget, Hope Lange, Millie Perkins, Donna Douglas, Barbara Eden, Judy Tyler, Teri Garr, Barbara McNair, Tuesday Weld, Ursula Andress) as well as veteran film stars (Barbara Stanwyck, Elsa Lanchester, Katy Jurado, Dolores Del Rio, Julie Adams, Lizabeth Scott, Stella Stevens, Angela Lansbury).

- Elvis' feature films grossed more than $180 million and are believed to have earned him over $20 million; 11 of his movie soundtrack albums went to the Top Ten, and of those, four went to Number 1.

- In a March, 1960, issue of *Life*, Elvis was quoted as saying, "I want to become a good actor, because you can't build a whole career on singing. Look at Frank Sinatra. Until he added acting to singing, he found himself slipping downhill."

- "The only thing worse than watchin' a bad movie is bein' in one." — *Elvis Presley*

Q. What was Hollywood like when you went out with Elvis in 1957?

A. I had been out there before, but staying with him was a different situation. We were at the Beverly Wilshire Hotel, Suite 850, in fact. Big four-bedroom suite. It was a 5,000-square-foot suite. He was making a tremendous amount of money. We could do anything we wanted to do.

Q. What happened when Elvis was asked to leave the Knickerbocker Hotel in Los Angeles?

A. They asked us to leave the Knickerbocker because we were throwing water into the peepholes and stuff like that. Just playing games. You knock on the door and throw a big thing of water through the keyhole. I mean, a thing like a peephole would be that big. You'd throw water in on somebody. It's just something to do. The Three Stooges, everybody used to stay there. You'd see them all, everybody. Everybody used to stay at the Knickerbocker. So he moved to the Beverly Wilshire right after we started *Jailhouse Rock*.

Q. Was Hollywood a real whirlwind for Elvis?

A. It was new to him. He had only done two pictures since he started. He had already done *Love Me Tender* and *Loving You*. The third picture was *Jailhouse Rock*. So he was just starting his motion picture career. They would give him his little setup for the next day, and he'd memorize the lines for that next day. He would memorize everybody else's lines. It was a situation of where that's what he enjoyed doing. He liked doing it.

Q. Did Elvis make a big impression with the established movie stars?

A. Yep. They all wanted to be around him. Sophia Loren came over to Paramount. Pat Boone would come over to sit and hang out. Bobby Darin. Elvis liked Bobby. He was doing *Jailhouse Rock*, and all these guys that I had watched all my life — Robert Taylor and Clark Gable and Glenn Ford and all these people — wanted to meet Elvis.

Yul Brynner and Danny Kaye, all these people. My God, it was just startling. Every time I turned around, there was a star that I had seen when I was a kid, so it was really shocking to me.

Glenn Ford would come over to the car and talk, and say, "How you doing, Lamar?" Yul Brynner and I got to be good friends. It was just really, you know, different. Nobody's prepared for that.

You could leave anytime you wanted to, but you were scared you were going to miss something. I think it was the routine that kept me stable.

Mitchum would come over. When I first met Bob Mitchum, it was in 1957. We were at the Beverly Wilshire Hotel. There was a knock on the door. I guess it was 9:30 or 10:00 at night. Banging on the door. That hallway in that hotel room had to be probably, I'd say, 50-60 feet long. I walked right down to the end of the hall and answered the door. It was Bob Mitchum. He had a fifth of Scotch. He said, "I want to talk to Elvis." I'm not going to tell Bob Mitchum he can't, big guy like he was. He came in. That's where I first met him.

He wanted Elvis to play his son in a picture that he did that he used his real son in, where he played a bootlegger. And Keely Smith was in it. He wanted Elvis to play his son. Elvis told him, "Mr. Mitchum, I'm sorry. I'm under contract to do another picture, and I can't." Mitchum was the type guy that just went to you and asked you. He didn't go to Colonel Parker. That's where I got to know Mitchum. He was really a super guy. And then, of course, Elvis met John Wayne. A bunch of them would come by the set and say hello to him and stuff like that. Jim Garner came over.

Q. Did Elvis ever meet James Dean?

A. No. He had a lot of James Dean's friends around him, like Nick Adams, a guy named Jack Simmons, Natalie Wood. Elvis had a group around him that knew Dean, and Elvis was fascinated with that. One of the reasons that he liked Nick and Natalie and these people was because they were friends of Jimmy Dean's. Elvis was fascinated with Jimmy Dean. Jimmy Dean was there before anybody was. He was the original rebel. And Elvis' music was the original rock 'n' roll.

Q. Did Elvis look up to Marlon Brando?

A. Oh, he liked Brando, yeah. He liked him. He thought Brando was fantastic. We were over at the Paramount lot when he was doing a picture with Karl Malden called *One-Eyed Jacks*.

The guy he liked better than anybody was Rod Steiger. Steiger would come backstage and see us, and we'd talk two or three hours to Steiger. Elvis liked Steiger as Al Capone.

Q. Did he ever connect with Brando over the years?

A. Never met him.

Q. Was there a particular place or time that Elvis socialized with the movie people?

A. We'd have touch football games every weekend at Beverly Glen Park. Everybody in the business, Ricky Nelson, everybody did it. Elvis had a team. His team was us, his friends from Memphis. That's where I got to know Bob Conrad. These different stars would come over and play. Played every Sunday down in the park. Crowds got so big we had to quit doing it.

It got tough. We knocked the shit out of each other. They used to run ringers in on it. They used to run part of the UCLA football team in on us. You'd get rough. Ricky Nelson would come down there with ringers. Kent McCord, the actor, from *Adam 12,* played. Boy, we'd be knocking the shit out of each other. I mean, it really got — Red and myself, when we hit people, I swear to God, it sounded like guns going off. Touch football can get rough. And Elvis wasn't untouchable. They'd knock the shit out of him. Whatever it was, he'd run the line. They'd hit him. Didn't make any difference. Elvis was rough and tumble. He used to get into it. Elvis was fast on his feet.

Q. Did it bother Elvis that he had to give up performing live in order to do films?

A. It did for the last four or five pictures, because he hated the pictures — he hated the songs. They were all formula pictures. And he hated those pictures. Elvis used to drink a lot of vodka before he'd go do a scene. He hated it. Singing to kids and dogs and stuff. He couldn't stand it.

Q. Was he punctual on the movie set?

A. We got there on time. He would show up on the set and have his lines memorized. We'd just sleep two or three hours and still get there. But I mean, back then, you're so young nothing phases you.

Q. Is it true Elvis was slated to do *A Star Is Born* with Barbra Streisand?

A. I was there when they met. She came over to see Elvis in Las Vegas and brought Jon Peters backstage. They had the option on *A Star Is Born*, so that's where that deal came down. Elvis said he'd agree to the deal, then he dumped it in the Colonel's lap, and it just never happened. Elvis was really excited, but it never worked out. The reason it didn't happen was because Colonel didn't want it to happen. Didn't like the billing. Elvis didn't either, for that matter.

Q. Did Elvis feel he was respected as an actor?

A. He always wanted to be a movie star. Elvis was a good actor. He really was. People didn't know that. He would have gotten better. He would have gotten a lot better. The worst thing Elvis had to get around was being Elvis. It was hard. I think eventually he'd have turned into a good actor. But I just never saw it happening, because it wasn't going to last.

Q. Did Elvis want to do more dramatic roles without singing?

A. Colonel convinced him, which is a fact, that if Elvis didn't do a song in a picture, he shouldn't do it. The picture he didn't do a song in, really, was one of the biggest flops he did. *Wild in the Country* just did not do anything. And Colonel used that on him forever. It just didn't do anything. After that, boy, I mean, everything changed. He went back to singing.

The movies got to be a joke. They really did. He hated doing them so bad. He couldn't stand doing those songs. He hated those songs. But Colonel had signed the deal, and Elvis had signed the contracts, so he had to do them or be in breach of contract.

Q. Did Elvis see his own movies?

A. He didn't go see his movies.

Q. Even the premieres?

A. There never was a premiere.

Q. Would he see the private showing?

A. Never saw it. Could care less.

Q. He'd be done and walk off the set?

A. That's it. A lot of actors are that way. Brando, De Niro, all of them. They won't go. Never go see the dailies. They don't want to see themselves.

Q. Was Elvis stigmatized in any way by his portrayal of a convict in *Jailhouse Rock*?

A. No.

Q. Did Elvis have friends in show business?

A. Elvis didn't have any show business friends. He did not have them. They didn't exist. Not a one. Nick Adams at the beginning, but Nick was going to do a picture with Tommy Sands. He wanted to find out what it was like being around us, so he did. But Elvis never had any acting friends. He liked Tom Jones. Tom and him got along real well. Tom was one of the few other entertainers that got into the inner circle.

Elvis could have really started his own Rat Pack if he wanted to, but he never did. He let Tom in. I'd say if anybody was ever inside the group, it would be Tom Jones. They connected in Hawaii. He came out to the house, and we'd go out and swim in the ocean and stuff like that. That's where Elvis and him bonded, really.

Q. Did Elvis admire other entertainers?

A. Elvis liked Tom Jones as a performer. He liked the way Tom moved, liked the way he sang. He genuinely liked Tom. Tom was doing a show. Elvis wasn't doing any shows. Elvis was only doing movies. And Tom Jones came along, and Elvis saw what he could be on stage again. He got jealous of that, so he got to know Tom. Started finding out what he was thinking about and stuff like that.

That's really what prompted Elvis getting back in the business, because we were doing nothing but movies, and Colonel wanted him to go back on the road, so we finished up that *Comeback Special*. After that, Colonel started setting up Vegas and everything else. That's when we started going back on the road. But Elvis appreciated the concerts. He appreciated what Tom was doing on stage. Elvis thought that Tom was the closest thing to him.

Q. Did Elvis ever see himself as a more contemporary Frank Sinatra?

A. Elvis was not as gregarious as Sinatra was. He was more shy than Sinatra. Sinatra came from a different era than Elvis did. Sinatra came back from the 1920s. You know, bathtub gin and speakeasies, stuff like that. Elvis was born in '35, you know, Second World War, and stuff like that. Sinatra was in his teens when Elvis was born. It was just a whole different era. Sinatra had a different attitude about stuff. He came from the Big Band Era.

Sinatra wanted to be Elvis' friend more than Elvis wanted to be Sinatra's. At the end, Frank was real close to Elvis. But earlier, Frank would call or one of his people would call and invite us to parties, and we wouldn't go. Elvis didn't want to hang around stars. He didn't like to do it. They bothered him. Frank's mother, Dolly, would come backstage to see Elvis. Elvis liked Dolly. He liked her a lot. He'd hug her and kiss her because she was round-faced like his mother. Dolly was a good person.

* * *

~ __Elvis and His Music__ ~

- "Gospel music was his first love." — *James Blackwood*

- "He taught white America to get down." — *James Brown*

- "If I could find a white man who had the Negro sound and the Negro feel, I could make a million dollars." — *Sam Phillips*

- "Rock 'n' roll music is basically gospel, rhythm-and-blues, or it sprang from that. And people have been adding things to it, experimenting with it." — *Elvis Presley*

Q. Is it true that when Elvis first walked into Sun Records, he really was more interested in sounding like Frank Sinatra or Dean Martin or one of the other pop crooners? That he hadn't found his own vocal style yet?

A. No. But Elvis didn't know what his style was right then. He developed it. He knew how to sing. He sang songs a certain way that he wanted to hear them sound. That was where he was different.

I mean, like *That's All Right, Mama* and *Blue Moon of Kentucky.* Nobody would have done *Blue Moon of Kentucky* like he did it. *Blue Moon of Kentucky* was bluegrass, real Kentucky bluegrass. Elvis did it rock 'n' roll. They said, "What the hell is that?" But this is what he picked up from black artists and gospel artists. He liked Bobby Blue Bland, and he liked Big Joe Turner.

Elvis was a meld of about two or three different styles. He liked opera. He liked R&B. He liked country. He listened to the *Grand Ole Opry* when he was like a kid in Mississippi. It all sort of melded. Elvis was a bucket. Everything was poured into it. That's why he ended up doing it that way.

He had certain voices that he copied, you know, Jake Hess and people like that. He grew up around gospel and thought Jake Hess was the greatest gospel singer that ever lived. Elvis' phrasing was Jake Hess' phrasing.

So as a consequence, as far as a style, his style developed after that. He had a style. In lieu of any other term, Elvis would be the "translator" for all these people rolled into one. But he was different. The reason he became Elvis Presley was because he had a style, but he didn't know that he had that.

Q. Did he ever talk about the power his music had over people?

A. I don't think the thought of what it did to people or anything else bothered him. It was just one of those things that started happening. He was selling records 90 miles a minute. He was going pretty fast. He didn't have time to think hardly at all. He was sort of the eye-of-the-storm, you know. It wasn't a case of what he thought about it. He didn't think much of anything. Elvis was very robotic, except when he got on stage.

Q. Did he have fun with his music?

A. Well, he liked it. He loved gospel and stuff like that. He and I would go through songs and hunt songs together. Things like that. But as far as fun with the music, sure, he enjoyed sessions and stuff like that. He was just getting into acting and he enjoyed that.

It was sort of really, just like I said, the eye-of-the-storm. It was one of those situations where this whirlwind was going around him. He really didn't think much of anything. Elvis just went out there and did it. Colonel got the dates for him, and he'd go do the dates.

Just like I said, he was really robotic about stuff. Elvis would say, "Just aim me somewhere, and I'll do it." That's just the way he was. He didn't do much complaining. He just did it. Colonel had everything set up for him, so he did. He didn't like a lot of hassle. At the end, you know, he was worn out and didn't like it. But at the beginning, it was all going pretty fast. It was incredible.

Q. What music did Elvis listen to?

A. Everything. He liked everything. He liked opera. He liked gospel. He liked rock 'n' roll. Liked R&B. There wasn't any music Elvis didn't like. He just liked music, period. Stuff he'd grown up with. The new stuff he would hear every once in a while, you know. Elvis didn't listen to the radio that much.

Q. Did Elvis believe his music was really good?

A. Yeah. At times he thought it was bad, because he wasn't getting good enough songs. But when he got good songs, he knew he was good. Elvis knew what he was. He knew what he could do. That was his job. It's like, you know, Jeff Gordon and these great Italian drivers and French drivers. They know who they are. They know what they do. They know not everybody can jump in that car and drive it. They know they can. That's what it was. Elvis was a gunslinger. He knew what he could do. He knew how fast he could draw.

Q. Did Elvis change his interpretation of a song every time he sang it?

A. He did. Interpretation would change every time he sang it. He'd hear something different, and he would change it.

Q. Did he sing with someone special in mind?

A. With *You Were Always on My Mind*, I think he'd remember Priscilla. I think that was part of that. Songs were his lifeblood. Elvis really always had a real strong emotional connection to a song, because he chose them.

Sinatra told me one time — Frank and I were talking about *My Way* — he said, "Lamar, that song was my song." He said, "Elvis does it, it becomes his."

I said, "Frank, that's why y'all are stylists." He said, "You're exactly right."

Frank said Elvis was one of the few people he'd ever seen that could take a song that everybody else did and make it his song. People associate *My Way* with Elvis as much as they do Frank.

Q. Did Elvis ever write a song?

A. He wrote one part of one song with Johnny Horton back in 1955. I don't know what it was.

Q. Was it ever recorded?

A. I think Horton recorded it. I'm not sure. No, Elvis never wrote a song.

Q. Did Elvis ever compose music?

A. No. Everything was acquired through other writers. We had a staff of great writers. Mort Shuman, Doc Pomus. Bobby Darin used to write for us and do demos. We had good guys, including all the Hill & Range writers. When it was time to record a song, Elvis would do the choosing. Then the producers would have to produce it.

When Eddie Rabbit wrote *Kentucky Rain*, I said, "This is a hit. I need to get it to Elvis." Eddie didn't want me to. I said, "You can take your choice here, Eddie." And Eddie used to tell this story on stage. He said, "Lamar told me, 'You can take a choice. You can do it and not make any money, or I can give it to Elvis and you'll make a fortune.'"

And that's how it happened with *Kentucky Rain*. I took it, and it came out of my office. That's how the songs got there. I knew that song was a hit for Elvis. It was. It was his last million seller.

Q. Did Elvis choose all his own songs to record?

A. Elvis chose everything. Elvis picked all his hits. Every song that ever hit, he picked. Between Freddie Bienstock and I, we would cull it from, like 500 songs, down to maybe 50 songs, and then Elvis would cull it from that to 50. Between Elvis and myself and Charlie Hodge and Red, we would cull it all the way down.

An example was the Memphis session in 1969. Marty Lacker was working for the producer Chips Moman, and Marty was the one who put that whole thing together. That's where Elvis got the best songs he ever got. *The Ghetto*, stuff like that, that came out of Memphis. That's where the good songs came from, and Marty got Elvis to come down there and do it.

That really revived Elvis' career at that point, Marty getting in the middle of it like that. All of us had really tremendous input to Elvis. We couldn't stop him from his drugs, but everything else we could do for him, we did.

Q. Was Elvis really focused on the lyrics of his songs and what they meant?

A. Oh, yeah. You just felt it. The music hits you and then the lyrics hit you. Everything has to tie together. That part I've never quite understood. I know hits when I hear them. I don't know how I know it. I just know it. That's my business. But you know it. You know it's there. He knew it. That was his business.

Q. How did Elvis' first Christmas album come about?

A. The one in 1957. He did it in July right before he played Hawaii. Colonel just told him, "It'd be a good thing to do a Christmas album."

Q. Did Elvis ever sit around the house and ever play an instrument?

A. He'd sit around the house and play the piano. He'd play the guitar, too. He'd sing and play some songs he was learning or something like that. He would always write it down. When Elvis wanted to learn a song, he would write it down. We'd put a record on. In Germany we'd do a lot of this. We'd put a record on and he would write the words down. Elvis would memorize songs by writing them down. Once he wrote them down, he'd get them. But he'd write them like a letter. He wouldn't write verse, chorus, verse. He would indicate going back to the chorus and stuff like that. When he wanted to memorize something, he would write it down.

Q. Was it mostly gospel music he did sitting around the house?

A. He loved gospel more than he did anything else. He'd sing gospel music. It was real easy for him. So he would do that. And certain songs he would do, too, on the piano and things like that. Gospel groups would come over every once in a while, but no, Elvis did not fool with his people, with his musician friends. Like the band and stuff like that, he didn't have them around that often. They were too different. They didn't run around with us. We didn't run around with them.

Q. Did Elvis listen to his own music?

A. At times, but very seldom.

Q. After Elvis became famous, did he ever go to his old haunts and sing?

A. Every once in a while, he did. We went and saw the Dixie Hummingbirds one time. Sat up in the balcony. He'd go backstage and do some of those gospel songs. At the Ellis Auditorium, he'd go back and sit in the wings. We'd see the show, watch the show from the wings.

Q. In the early days, before Elvis appeared on TV and was known only on radio and records, people thought he was black?

A. Everybody did. Elvis loved black churches. Yeah, he would go watch the Dixie Hummingbirds, the Five Blind Boys.

Q. How did that impact on a daily basis? Did you ever have the Ku Klux Klan or other racist groups show up?

A. No, no, no. Never, no. Nothing like that ever happened. It was kind of like being in a balloon. A balloon rides in the wind, not in front of it or behind it, and that's where we were with Elvis. We were in a balloon. We were in the wind. We were not in front of it or behind it. We were moving along with it. That's why in your balloon you can talk to people on the ground, like we're talking right now, and they can hear every word you're saying, because you're in the wind. You're inside of it. Elvis was inside of the wind. He was inside of it, not in front of it or behind it. He was inside of it. And it moved with him.

Q. So you never had any problems in terms of racial issues? People coming up and saying "This is forbidden music" or anything like that?

A. Never. No. Blacks loved him. Oh, they loved him. Elvis never had an integration problem. It never existed. He loved black music. He'd go listen to it. Elvis loved blues and country. That's where all the melting pot came. Elvis listened to B.B. King's show on WDIA, the black station. It was a clear channel, but it was a directional antenna that went out of Memphis. You could hardly pick it up that well in Memphis. You could, but not that well. It was a 50,000-watt directional antenna directed down toward the south. We used to listen to it all the time. Elvis had no prejudice. He didn't have any prejudice. It didn't bother him. It wasn't a big deal.

B.B. King had a label called Blues Boy Records. That's where he got the name B.B. His real name is not B.B. He was called the Blues Boy, and that's where his name B.B. King came from. Sam Phillips at Sun Records recorded people like Little Junior Parker, Bobby Blue Bland and these people. Elvis was the first white artist Sam ever heard that sang black music. See, that's where that whole thing came about. That's why for a long time everybody thought Elvis was black. He wasn't, he was white. He had grown up listening to black rhythm-and-blues, so he imitated it.

Q. What were Elvis' favorite songs?

A. He liked *Are You Lonesome Tonight?*. He loved that. He liked *I'll Remember You*, the Kui Lee song. He loved that one. There were about four or five songs he liked.

Q. Who brought Mickey Newbury's *An American Trilogy* to Elvis?

A. I brought *American Trilogy* to him … and he did it. That was the only thing he ever did of Mickey's.

Q. Did you also bring *Hound Dog* to him?

A. No. He found *Hound Dog* when he was walking in the Sahara Hotel in Las Vegas. There was a group called Freddie Bell and The Bellboys. They were doing a Big Mama Thornton song written by Jerry Leiber and Mike Stoller. Elvis heard it. He told Freddie, "I want that song." That's how that song got to him. He found it. Freddie Bell and The Bellboys were doing it first.

Q. What songs did you give to Elvis over the years?

A. He got about eight or nine hits out of my office. *Kentucky Rain* was one, from a writer I signed named Eddie Rabbit. It became Elvis' fiftieth gold record and another million seller. Got Elvis to do *Indescribably Blue, True Love Travels on a Gravel Road*, a lot of the country stuff. Quite a few. Mort Shuman, Doc Pomus stuff. It was good to be able to contribute to Elvis' creative process.

Q. Did Elvis like Nashville?

A. He didn't like Nashville that well. He didn't care for it. Elvis single-handedly, boy, when he hit, he wiped out country music for about two years. The markets went to hell. He killed it. But Elvis liked country music.

Q. Did it bother Elvis being called a "living legend" and "the King of Rock 'n' Roll"?

A. No, he didn't pay any attention to it. He never paid any attention to it.

* * *

~ **Elvis and Priscilla** ~

- November, 1959: Elvis is introduced at an Army party in Germany to Priscilla Ann Beaulieu, 14-year-old daughter of an Air Force captain; they meet again in December, 1960, when Elvis convinces Priscilla's parents to let her spend Christmas with him at Graceland; starting in October, 1962, she is a permanent guest at Graceland and at Elvis' home in Bel Air, California.

- September, 1966: *Weekend* publishes rumor of Elvis and Priscilla's elopement; on Christmas Eve, Elvis formally proposes; May 1, 1967: Elvis and Priscilla marry in a private ceremony at the Aladdin Hotel, Las Vegas.

- February 1, 1968: Lisa Marie Presley is born, Elvis' only known child.

- February 23, 1972: Elvis and Priscilla separate; divorce granted, October 9, 1973.

Q. Did the Colonel pressure Elvis to marry Priscilla to avoid a scandal like what had happened with Jerry Lee Lewis marrying his cousin?

A. The Colonel had quite a bit to do with it, in fact. I think Elvis would have stayed single all his life, outside of maybe the fact of wanting to have a child. That's one of the reasons he got married, but he didn't really need to get married. Marriage never fitted him.

Q. Did Priscilla have knowledge of Elvis' drug use when they were first married?

A. Oh, yeah. We all did. Hell, I spent their honeymoon with them. We had a trailer there on the ranch, the Circle G Ranch. And Elvis and Priscilla were in the back bedroom of the trailer and I was in the front bedroom of the trailer. Elvis said, "I'm going to write a book on how Lamar spent my honeymoon with us." Priscilla married the group. She didn't marry him. She married the whole group. She didn't like it, I don't think.

Q. How did Elvis find out about Priscilla's affair with Mike Stone?

A. We found out in the group, and then he started finding out about it. When it all started coming down, it was horrible. It wasn't her messing around on him that pissed him off. What pissed him off was she had the effrontery to do it. He just could not get over her doing that to him, yet it was okay for him to do it but not okay for her. It's that old Southern thing. What's fair for the goose is definitely not fair for the gander. That's what really tore him up. He couldn't believe she would do that, and that got him pissed off.

Q. Did his concern over the affair affect the music at some point?

A. No, it never affected the music. He'd sing more ballads, you know, *You're Always on My Mind* and stuff like that. But it was a melancholy period, of course. Sure, everybody goes through that. He would express it in his songs, but it wasn't any big going out in the street and having to drink and cry. That never happened. It was within the group that he would get messed up and get mad at us, stuff like that. It was tough on us, but it was always tough on us.

Q. When you first heard about the affair with Mike Stone, what did you think was going to happen? Did you think she and Elvis would reconcile?

A. No. I knew it was over with.

Q. Did he ever go into a rage and actually confront her?

A. He used to go nuts. Go insane. He'd go out of his mind.

Q. Is there truth to the rumor that he would chase her around the house with a gun?

A. No. No. He never chased her around the house with a gun. No, that never happened. Absolutely not. He wouldn't confront her that much with it. Elvis, like I told you, was non-confrontational. He gave her quite a bit of money and stuff like that.

Q. How did Priscilla meet Mike Stone?

A. Mike Stone was a bodyguard for Phil Spector. They came backstage, Phil did. Phil talked to me. He said, "Can I meet Elvis?" I said, "Sure, Phil." So I brought Phil, and Mike was his bodyguard. I brought them backstage. And that's when they got attracted to each other. That's the first time she had ever met Mike. So that's how it all came about. Then she started taking karate lessons from Mike. Everything went from there.

Q. Truth or myth: Elvis seriously entertained the idea of killing Mike Stone at the time?

A. Oh, I think it was a lot of bravado there. I think that, you know, you say, "I'll have him killed." Well, that's bullshit. When you're getting ready to take somebody's life, it all changes.

Q. A hit man, the actual person, had been arranged to kill Mike Stone?

A. The man was already hired. The guy [hit man] was ready to go do it. He had called from a phone booth. We went and talked to Elvis. Said, "You're getting ready to make a big mistake here." And he backed off.

Q. Who had arranged that?

A. I'll never say his name. He was another actor. Very famous actor, in fact.

Q. After Elvis died, did the estate try to sanitize his image?

A. Well, I think, you know, anybody tries to do that. People want you to hear the good, not the bad. The estate was not in good shape after he died. Elvis went through money. I'm glad Priscilla got it. They rolled their sleeves up and brought the estate back around, her and her advisors. That's what brought it back around. Controlling an image is a tough business.

Q. Do you remember much about Lisa Marie from her childhood?

A. I was there when she was born. I knew her up until she was about five or six years old and even nine, the age she was when Elvis died. She didn't talk much. Not to us. She didn't have much to say. She was always a very quiet person. But I hear she's just about as hard-headed as he was. She's single-minded. She does what she wants.

Q. Did Elvis have other children than Lisa Marie?

A. No. No. No, absolutely not. There's many of them claim that they're his daughter or son. He'd have had to be the father of our country, wouldn't he? Elvis didn't screw around. He didn't. He played around, but he didn't have intercourse. Lisa Marie was it. He was very, very safe about that. He'd use condoms and stuff like that. Elvis was very careful. Didn't want those problems and never had them.

Q. Did Elvis express a desire for having additional children?

A. He always wanted a son, and he never got one. Would have been interesting if he had one. He had a name picked out, even: John Baron Presley.

* * *

~ <u>Elvis</u> <u>and</u> <u>His</u> <u>Other</u> <u>Women</u> ~

- July 19, 1954: the first-ever copy of an Elvis Presley record was purchased at Charles Records, Memphis, by a 15-year-old girl, Eldene Beard.

- "My heart was racing just seeing him up onstage. I felt like tearing his pelvis off."
  — *Woman at an Elvis concert, Las Vegas, 1969*

- "I knew the first time I met him that he was not like other people." — *Dixie Locke, Elvis' girlfriend, Memphis, 1953*

Q. Did Elvis think of himself as a sex symbol?

A. No. Don't get me wrong. He knew who he was. Elvis never at any given time did not know who he was. He knew he was good looking. He knew what he had going. If he didn't, he would have been an idiot. But he knew. Sure, he knew who he was. But there was no one like him at all in that day. He was the first. He was what every girl wanted and wanted their boyfriends to be and didn't have guts enough to tell them, "Damn it, get like Elvis!".

Q. Truth or myth? In an attempt to get Elvis to do a movie with her, Jayne Mansfield slept with him for three days, whereupon he said, "But it's the Colonel who makes these decisions, not me."?

A. Never happened. Elvis didn't like big tits. He's an ass/leg man.

Q. Was there ever a woman he really wanted yet never had a relationship with?

A. No, I can never think of one.

Q. Was Ann-Margret one of his true loves?

A. He loved Ann, yeah. I think Ann would have been, but Ann wouldn't give up her career. She was very career-oriented. Elvis believed in that old Southern routine that "you stay at home, I'll take care of everything else", and Ann wasn't going to do that. They were really in love with each other, so it became a situation where I think had Ann given up her career and everything, he would have married her, but she wasn't going to do that. It wouldn't have worked.

Q. While Priscilla and Elvis were engaged, was she aware of his relationship with Ann-Margret?

A. Elvis managed to keep it under wraps for a long time, because Priscilla was in Memphis and he was in Los Angeles making movies. Elvis would go out with Ann and insist on going out without the guys for protection. This bothered everybody. He'd pick her up in a Rolls Royce, and they'd go riding around.

Q. What was Elvis' relationship with Nancy Sinatra?

A. When we came back from Germany, Nancy Sinatra met him and gave him a present, because Elvis was going to do the Frank Sinatra show in Miami. Nancy was never a girlfriend. He liked Nancy. Frank would come over and stuff like that. But they got along okay. Nancy was a good girl.

Q. Is it true that girls would come out to Graceland and he would pick which one he wanted? Then it was open game for the rest of you?

A. Yeah. It's the truth, yeah. It worked that way all the time. You know, we'd find out whoever he wanted and we'd make a place for the rest of them. That's just part of it. That's called rock 'n' roll, isn't it?

Q. Did you have any problem with him stealing girls away that you guys were trying to meet?

A. No. He always got them first. There was too many of them to go around. It was never one girl. It was a group.

Q. Was he ever rejected by a woman?

A. No. He got upset with Ann-Margret because Ann wouldn't go his route, but Elvis just broke it off. He would just break it off. That was the end of it. When he broke it off with a girl, he never saw her or talked to her again.

Elvis could handle women better than anybody I've ever known in my life. Every one would get around Elvis, and they'd want to nurse him. They wanted to take care of him like he was a little kid or something. Damnedest thing I've ever seen. Women would go nuts over him. They all wanted to help him. He was Mr. Helpless. Here was a guy making 25-30 million a year being helpless, right?

Q. And they were going to save him?

A. Oh, from himself. He'd let them think that.

Q. Post-divorce, is it true Elvis saw his girlfriends as substitutes for Priscilla?

A. No. He never saw anybody as a substitute for her.

Q. Why did Linda Thompson finally leave?

A. The isolation of the whole thing. Elvis was a person who loved isolation. He loved being the enigma that he was. The reason he was that is because he did certain things he didn't want people to know what he was doing. She got tired of it all. You don't get out in the public. You don't know what's going on. She had other things in her life that she wanted to do. She started dating a piano player. Elvis found out about that, so that started breaking it off.

Linda was the best one he ever had. Linda's done very well for herself. She's a very single-minded, smart, intelligent, lovely woman. She was the best thing that Elvis had. We've often thought, and I said it a long time, that he'd have still been alive had she been there. Because she would go in and check on him.

Q. Did Elvis choose Ginger Alden because she reminded him physically of Priscilla?

A. She was young-looking. She was a pretty girl, young. He liked young girls. He always did that. But I don't think he'd have ever married her. She claimed he would have, but I'm pretty sure he wouldn't have. Elvis, he'd promise a girl anything.

* * *

~ **Elvis and His Main Men**: The **Memphis Mafia** ~

AS ELVIS MADE his rapid ascent into super-stardom, his casual friends and running buddies evolved into a close-knit cadre of confidants, bodyguards, valets and advance men.

The Memphis Mafia provided insulation from the demands of the outside world as well as emotional support for a shy, insecure young man who just a few years before had been ridiculed by his teen peers for the unique character qualities that now made him one of the most envied people on the planet.

Though he had given up control of his business affairs to Colonel Parker, Elvis maintained total control over public access to his private life — at least until 1977, when Memphis Mafia members Red West, Sonny West and Dave Hebler wrote *Elvis: What Happened?*, a behind-the-scenes account of the singular personal and professional world of Elvis Presley.

Q. Did the Memphis Mafia evolve specifically because of Elvis' sudden celebrity?

A. One minute a person is living a normal life. The next minute they're in this celebrity arena. They need normal people to be with them to just keep in touch with who they are. He kept a group around him for that reason. Elvis wasn't friendly with a lot of people. The reason was because he was so terribly shy, and around us, he didn't have to be that way.

But outside of our circle, Elvis didn't make friends. Other actors, they never could understand Elvis. It was not a case that he didn't like them. He just didn't want to know them. He didn't care. He was really jealous of us. I was friends with Frank Sinatra, and I was friends with Sammy Davis, Jr., and Elvis was very jealous of that. He didn't like it. He said, "They don't pay you. I do."

Q. So the Memphis Mafia served as a shield for his eccentricities?

A. The inner circle kept the public from seeing the star's whole personality. They saw a nice guy. He built his own world around him, and that's who he trusted, that's who he bullshitted with and that's who he beat to death. And the outside world saw him as a cherub, and he wasn't. Listen, he was mean when he wanted to be. But the last year of his life, Elvis was never outside the circle. He was so messed up that we had to keep him inside.

Q. Did you originally come up with the phrase "Memphis Mafia"?

A. No. Some newspaper people in Las Vegas came up with it. That's how it stuck to us from then on out. Marty Lacker and I and Billy Smith, we locked it. Yeah, we own it. I still own a third of it. Marty and Billy sold their two-thirds, but I still own my third.

Q. Who would you define as the core Memphis Mafia?

A. The immediate group is Red West, Sonny West, Marty Lacker, Billy Smith and myself.

Q. Red West was the one that took up for Elvis during a fight in high school, right?

A. Red just told the guy, said, "You gotta whip me first." Elvis never forgot Red for that. Red was real close. Red was very close to him.

Q. Were other people admitted to the core group as years went by?

A. Elvis would bring new guys in, because new guys, he could smoke them, but us, he couldn't. He'd blow smoke up their ass. He couldn't blow it up ours, because we knew him. He just liked certain people around him.

We'd joke about it. We'd be on a boat, and the boat wouldn't be close to the dock. I'd just tell him to walk to the dock, walk across the water and walk up to the dock. He'd say, "What do you mean?" I'd say, "Well, I'm sure you can do that, too." I'd do it to deflate him, you know. Got him pretty mad.

That's the reason Elvis started putting younger guys into the group, because he could influence them. He couldn't us. We were the old hands. We knew what he was doing. So he would get younger guys in. He'd smoke them big time. We'd just walk around going, "Gee whiz," you know.

Q. If Elvis liked you, you were a fully admitted member of the circle?

A. Oh, yeah. Oh, absolutely. Certainly. If Elvis decided to buy himself a new Cadillac, he would buy all of the guys new Cadillacs too.

Q. After a certain point were you there not because of the excitement, not because of the money, but because you really loved Elvis?

A. We were all there for that. We were just so much a part of him. I think a lot of his personality came from us and ours from him. I still do things today that he used to do that I, you know, don't even know I'm doing it. I was around him so long. Like how I play the guitar and going out and buying too much of this. Things that just happen, because you had such a sheltered existence with this one group of people.

Q. After the publication of the first "insider" book, *Elvis: What Happened?*, how angry was Elvis?

A. Real angry. He went bananas, because it was the first time the veil of secrecy was lifted, and he didn't like that. He didn't like it at all. You hear people say, "It caused Elvis to die." It didn't cause Elvis to die. It upset him. Yeah, he hated it. And Sonny had thought that it would wake him up, but it did the opposite. It lifted a veil of secrecy he didn't like, and Elvis was determined to keep that secrecy no matter what.

Stuff goes on with every star that people don't know. That's what you try to keep private. Well, today, that veil is very thin. In fact, now it's worse. It's thinner than tissue paper. But back then we could control it.

Q. Are you all still in frequent contact with each other?

A. If nothing else, Elvis put one hell of a group together. We're all really to this day extremely close. We're like brothers, Red and I and Billy and Marty are, and Sonny. I've tried to get a reunion together two or three times. You can't. Our group, we get together and talk. We talk to each other. Marty calls. We talk every day. Red calls me once a week. We all talk.

It's taken a long time for everybody to get over it. There's a lot of us still hadn't got over it. We still do things that are not, you know, normal. We all suffered what they call post-traumatic stress syndrome. The others, they all understand, because they were on the inside. They know what we all go through. It was one of those situations of where, because it was such a long ride that when it stopped, it was like — hell, my ears rang for two years. They say it's not how fast you go, it's how quick you stop. And boy, let me tell you something, we stopped real quick.

Q. Are there secrets among the group that haven't yet come out?

A. We know everything Elvis did. And there are certain things we'll never, ever talk about. If we ever pull the lid off, this country will go crazy. We wrote our own laws. Always remember that. We did. We could do anything we wanted to do anytime, anywhere, anyplace. Nobody ever bothered us. Anywhere we were was a sanctuary. Nobody messed with us — never, ever. We got away with murder. We didn't murder anybody, but we got away with everything else.

* * *

~ **Elvis and His Public** ~

- January, 1961: Elvis is denied admission to UCLA because university officials fear his presence on campus will be disruptive.

- August, 1965: Elvis entertains the Beatles at his home in Bel Air; the Beatles ask Elvis if he wants to be the "fifth Beatle".

- December, 1970: Elvis drops in on President Nixon at the White House and volunteers to become a "Federal Agent at Large".

- January, 1971: Elvis is named one of Ten Most Outstanding Young Men of America by U.S. Jaycees.

- December, 1972: Elvis reportedly gives more than $100,000 to children's charities at Christmas; during his lifetime, he made an estimated $20 million in charitable donations.

Q. Did Elvis like the public contact that came with touring?

A. He loved touring. He loved being in front of people. He loved his fans. Elvis was very loyal to his fans. He liked to play in front of them, but he didn't like to be around them. There's a difference. It's like a gunslinger. If they don't have the guns on, you never see them. But they put their guns on, you just stay out of their way. Because he got on the stage and that was his medium. But he didn't like to be around them.

He liked to see them. He liked for them to see him. He'd do a show. That's the end of it. He didn't want to be around them. He didn't want to be around anybody at anytime. He was not a hanger-outer. He just didn't do it.

Q. Did Elvis express wonder or irritation about his fans?

A. He'd think sometimes they wanted too much. He'd say, "What do they want from me? They're getting everything they can get. I can't give them anymore." Elvis would relate to a Paul Newman picture called *Cool Hand Luke*. He loved it. Paul Newman's character said, "Everybody just leave me alone." You remember when he went nuts and everything? He said, "You're sucking me dry."

That's what Elvis felt. He felt everybody was just pulling on him. He said, "I'm tried of people pulling on me. Everybody is pulling on me. I'm tired of it. Quit living vicariously through me." He would say it in press conferences. He said, "I am who I am. Don't live through me. Live through somebody else. Don't live through me."

Q. What about when he was in Hollywood doing films?

A. On the sets he was very quiet. Elvis was a really shy person. He was only comfortable around people he knew, and that was us. He wasn't comfortable around anybody else. He'd meet another star and get very uncomfortable. He just didn't like it. He was out of his element. They all wanted to see him. He didn't want to see them.

Q. When he would come in the room, would the whole room tense up?

A. Sure, all the time with Elvis. He'd walk in the room. He'd change the whole room. We would have parties in the group, and we wouldn't invite him because he would ruin the party. Everybody would go over to his side of the room and talk to him. We'd be standing there like idiots. So we never would invite him. He used to get mad about it. He said, "Y'all won't invite me to your parties." We said, "We don't want you. You take the party up. You ruin the party. We don't want you there."

Q. Did he always have that special electricity?

A. Oh, he always had it, yeah. He could walk into a room, and you with your back turned, and you'd instantly know he was in the room.

Q. Did Elvis like doing press interviews?

A. He disliked interviews. It just wore him out. Nobody came up with any original questions. It was always the same. There were no original questions. Very seldom did you get an original question. It just didn't happen. The only one was from Wolfman Jack that time. It hit him so left field, about what it was like to be Elvis. Elvis asked me, "What do you think?" I said, "I don't know. You're talking about you, not me."

Q. Did Elvis have any involvement in politics?

A. No. Had nothing to do with it. Didn't like it.

Q. Did anyone ever solicit him as a candidate?

A. No.

Q. Did Elvis go out in public wearing disguises?

A. No. Elvis couldn't disguise himself. He'd come down with like a pimp coat on and a long-brimmed hat. He'd say, "Nobody will ever recognize me." I'd say, "You're going out here tonight dressed like that?" He thought that was a disguise. There was no way. You couldn't disguise him. He wouldn't go disguised anyway, because he was scared somebody wouldn't recognize him.

Q. Was it a rare occasion that he went off by himself?

A. Not very often, but he would do it. He'd go to downtown Memphis by himself on a motorcycle ride. He'd do it with Ann-Margret, get the Rolls Royce and drive over to scc Ann. He and Ann would go riding around.

Q. Do you think it got to a point in his career that a majority of people wanted Elvis to fail and took pleasure in his troubles?

A. Everybody wants everybody to fail. Nobody wants anybody to win. I used to go fishing as a kid and I used to get crawdads. You catch crawdads, and then you use them to catch fish. You put them in a bucket. One of them will try to crawl out and another one will reach up and pull him back in. Same routine. That's the way it is. Nobody wants to see anybody succeed. In my life, I've always wanted to see everybody make it. When somebody makes money, I think it's the greatest thing in the world, because I've been on the inside and I've seen what it takes to do it.

But people like to see people fail. They love it. Why do you think people go to races? They don't go to see the car go round and round and round. Why do people go to boxing matches? Nobody wants to see people make it. They want it, but they don't want it. It's a contradiction in human nature.

Q. Is the story about him giving a Cadillac to a stranger truth or myth?

A. Truth. Elvis' generosity was well-documented, even his gifts to strangers. He was buying cars one day, and this old woman was outside looking in at the window. He walked up to her. He said, "What are you looking at?" She said, "I'm looking at that convertible. Been looking at that Cadillac there." And he said, "It's yours." And he gave it to her. That happened at the Cadillac dealership down on Union. That actually happened.

He would give stuff away all the time. I'm talking about the Elvis museums and stuff like that. There's so much stuff out there that Elvis gave away. Elvis was one of the most generous human beings that ever lived. That's why there's so much stuff out there on Elvis, because he gave so much stuff away. Elvis was probably one of the greatest consumers that ever lived. He once said to me, "The great thing about giving a car to someone, you don't have to worry about it fitting."

Q. Why this mania for consumption?

A. Elvis was very wealthy. Elvis was the highest paid performer of his time.

Q. Did Elvis want to buy a helicopter?

A. He was going to get one, just never got around to it. He'd have eventually got one.

Q. Did other pop musicians frequently try to visit him?

A. One time, Led Zeppelin wanted to meet Elvis. We were playing that big venue there in L.A., the Forum. And they all came over. Elvis asked me, "What do they do?" I said, "They're singers, a group." He didn't know who they were. He just did not know. Did not know Led Zeppelin, Jimmy Page. Didn't know any of them. But they came up there, and Elvis talked, and they talked a while. But he didn't know who they were. Could care less. A few years before, the Beatles came by the house in L.A.

Q. When Elvis flew to Washington and saw President Nixon, why didn't he use one of his planes instead of flying on a commercial liner?

A. He got on a plane by himself. He had on a suit. It was like a furry suit or something. I can't remember what it was. But he got on the plane and went by himself. Elvis walked up to the gates of the White House, to the security, said, "I'm Elvis. I want to meet President Nixon." The guys didn't know what to do. They panicked. They called up and got Egil Krogh, who was an aide to Nixon. Krogh came down and there was Elvis. He said, "Come on." So Nixon canceled out three appointments to meet him. Everyone at Graceland was frantic because they didn't know where he was. Nobody knew where he was. He had just left.

He called me on the way back. I was coming back from a deer hunt. Ray Baker was with me and Dallas Frazier. Elvis got on the phone and he said, "Lamar, meet me in Nashville." I said, "Where are you?" He said, "Where are you?" I said, "I'm about 60 miles outside of Nashville. Come on to the airport."

And I said, "Okay. I'll meet you at the plane. What do you want? I'm going to need to go home and change." He said, "No, come on like you are." And I had been hunting deer for two or three days and the whole thing. I drove out to the airport.

He had me get on the plane with him and fly to Memphis. He told me he couldn't wait to tell me the whole story.

* * *

~ **The Everyday Elvis** ~

- March, 1966: Elvis and Memphis Mafia members Sonny West and Jerry Schilling file a formal UFO sighting, claiming to have seen an extra-terrestrial object from Elvis' home in Bel Air.

- January, 1967: Elvis meets Dr. George Nichopoulos ("Dr. Nick"), a Memphis physician who in the next ten years will supply Elvis with prescription drugs on demand, an estimated 19,000-plus pills in the last two years of Elvis' life.

- Summer, 1971: in response to anonymous threats on Priscilla and Lisa Marie, Elvis hires armed guards to protect his family.

- "I've always lived a straight, clean life." — *Elvis Presley*

Q. Did Elvis gamble?

A. He never gambled. He had no interest in it at all. His mind never went that direction. He'd bet $500 or something just for the hell of it, but he never would gamble. He never did gamble. Never did.

Q. Did Elvis ever have any problems with the IRS?

A. Elvis? No. Never, ever.

Q. Did Elvis read a lot of classic literature, so-called "great books"?

A. As far as reading the great books, no, he never read them. He didn't know any of that. He didn't know who Homer was. He didn't know Mark Twain. He knew who Mark Twain was, because he'd heard about it when he was in high school. But he didn't know it.

Q. Did Elvis watch the news on television?

A. Sometimes he would, yeah. Elvis liked to watch TV. Had Elvis lived where we have cable now, he never would have come out of that bedroom. He'd still be up there. In fact, that's probably what he's doing now. He's got the Great Cable now.

He had one single TV in front of him. That's what he would watch. He would watch different channels. His attention span wouldn't last that long. We had it on because we watched it. At our parties we'd turn the TV on and turn the sound off. Just something was going all the time.

Q. Where would the parties at Graceland take place?

A. The parties started off in the basement, then moved to the den. Graceland's not a big house. It's not a big house at all. What it is, is a Greek revival house, and it's just not that big. All the ancillary houses around it and everything makes it a fairly big estate, but not the estate itself. That house, I'd say, is probably 5,000, maybe 6,000 square feet total.

Q. Was Christmas Elvis' favorite time of year?

A. Definitely! He had an excuse for giving gifts, you know. And he liked playing Santa Claus. But Elvis gave all the time. That's just something he did. He just liked to do it. He always gave. He'd give you a car or a truck, because you didn't have to take it back, because you didn't have a problem with it fitting. It always fit.

Q. Did Elvis give to charities?

A. Yes, he was very generous. He had a whole group of charities that he'd give to every year. He loved the March of Dimes. Elvis thought that money was going out of season at dark, so he just got rid of it all. He gave enormous amounts of money and cars and things. Elvis, that was his thing. He was a very generous person.

He gave a yacht to Danny Thomas and St. Jude's Hospital. Elvis liked St. Jude's. He gave a lot to St. Jude's. It was a presidential yacht. We went onboard. It had Einstein's telegram to Franklin Roosevelt that read "I have discovered atomic fusion." And "E=mc2" was in the telegram.

Elvis bought the yacht. Colonel painted one side of it, the side that faced the dock. Elvis bought it in an auction. Colonel bought it, in actuality, in Elvis' name. And Elvis turned around and gave it to Danny Thomas, and Danny Thomas sold it for the hospital. But it was a presidential yacht. In other words, all the presidents used it, not only Roosevelt, but other ones too.

Q. Was there some reason why Elvis consistently bought Cadillacs?

A. Just liked them. He bought a '55 Cadillac and had it painted pink for his mother. He had Cadillacs and Lincolns. He had a Continental Mark II. He had a lot of Lincolns.

Q. Did Elvis have consistent nightmares?

A. Yes, people coming after him and stuff like that, people attacking him. He had those all his life. The more famous he got, the more they were attacking him. That was his thing. That was his paranoia. Gladys had the nightmares, too. The whole family did. Vernon and Gladys had them. It was a family trait, I think. Gladys asked me, "Will you sleep in there with him?" I said, "Yeah, I guess so." And I did, to keep him from hurting himself. That bed was as big as this room. She told me about the nightmares, told me what to do when Elvis had them.

Q. Did he get physically out of control at night?

A. Oh, yeah. He flailed and struck out. He would wake up in the middle of the night, hit me in the jaw, knock me clean out of the bed. As I was falling out of the bed, I flipped the light, and he woke up and started laughing. His mother always told me, "If you'll turn the light on, he's okay." And I've had him hit me in the back of the head with me crawling toward the light to turn it on.

So finally, to keep from getting hurt, I would move down. I put a pallet down at the end of the bed so I could duck and dive. Because I wouldn't sleep with him. I said, "I can't sleep up here with you. You drive me crazy. You toss and turn. I go to sleep. You hit me. I can't put up with this." So I put a pallet down at the end of the bed. Then after I'd take all the girls home, I'd come back upstairs. He wouldn't go to bed until I got back up there.

In '57-'58, the sleep walking was real bad … '56-'57, it was really, really bad. In the service, it was fairly bad, but I'd come in and wake him up. It went away later on, but still every once in a while, he'd have the nightmares.

Q. Were the nightmares increased by Elvis' sudden fame?

A. Yes. We were not prepared for it. We had no reason to be prepared for it. I didn't know anything about it. I knew I wanted to be with him, but I had no reason to prepare for it. I got in the middle of it and I said, "Good God Almighty!" It was unbelievable.

Q. Was Elvis an insomniac?

A. He was an insomniac all his life. Elvis was not a long sleeper. We'd go to sleep 4:00, 5:00, 6:00 in the morning. Sleep to about 2:00 or 3:00 in the afternoon. We were like bats. Sunlight would come in. We'd go hide somewhere. Most entertainers, road dogs are that way. I mean, you know, Mick Jagger to this day probably sleeps until noon. That's just part of your life. It's your lifestyle. It's like you're on the nightshift. Elvis hated performing matinees. Could not stand matinees. Talked to him one day, he said, "You tell Colonel if he sets me another matinee, I'm not going to do it." And I told Colonel, "You need to cut these matinees." Because Elvis didn't like waking up to do them. He didn't like it.

Q. Was Elvis physically incapacitated toward the end?

A. No.

Q. Is it true his poor health got to the point you guys were carrying him around the house?

A. Never happened.

Q. Truth or myth: Elvis was so drugged up that he'd pass out in his food?

A. He did that a lot of times. He would be eating, and the downers, I mean, the sleeping pills, he'd just fall in his plate. I've seen him fall face first in the damn bowl of mashed potatoes and gravy. Just, boom! You had to pick him up and clean his face off.

Q. In the earlier days, did you all consume drugs with Elvis?

A. Sure. In the later days, I grew out of it. I got tired of it. We got into coke. I loved that. I thought it was great when we got into coke. But Elvis didn't like it that much, because it was an upper. He liked downers.

Q. Were you guys consuming a lot?

A. Quite a bit. Elvis got into liquid coke. He'd put it on swabs and stick them up his nose. These long cotton things. And you'd stay high for three, four, five hours. You know, ripped.

Q. How long would he go sometimes without sleeping?

A. You mean all of us? We've gone four or five days without sleep.

Q. Was that with taking uppers?

A. Yeah, sure.

Q. Was it taking handfuls at that time or in moderation?

A. Elvis never did anything in moderation.

Q. Was the whole crew taking the pills?

A. We were all, yeah.

Q. Did Elvis require that?

A. No. We just decided we wanted to do it. Didn't have to require nothing. But in the latter part of Elvis' life, he went into downers. He liked downers. He was a downer freak, Dilaudid and Demerol, stuff like that. He loved it. Because he'd just get really messed up. He wouldn't eat. I've seen him go through a whole, big tray of popsicles. He'd put them on a platter and eat the whole thing. Because, you know, that's the only thing he could tolerate on his stomach. When you're into serious narcotics, you can't eat. You have to have sugar.

Q. When did Elvis become heavily involved in the downers?

A. It shifted in the middle part of the '70s. He liked Dilaudid and stuff like that. I told him what Dilaudid was one time, and he got mad at me. He said, "You know what? You are fired for that." And I said, "Okay". This was one of our big fights.

Dilaudid is the last thing they give you before you die of cancer. The terminal pain, it takes it away. Boy, I mean, it is strong. Elvis used to get it and knock a hole in his hand and wouldn't even know it. He had different drugs. Seconal, Tuinal, stuff like that in it. Just different mixtures, cocktails. The Dilaudid he shot straight into his hip. The nurse would do that.

Q. Why did Elvis have the upstairs at Graceland closed off?

A. He had it closed off because he didn't want anybody up there. That became his whole refuge, that whole upstairs. He took over the whole upstairs. That was his domain up there. He could wander around and nobody would bother him. He'd stay up there for months on end. I've seen him stay up there for two or three months at a time. Never come down.

Q. Did Elvis have a nurse with him 24 hours a day?

A. Yeah, he did. For about four or five years, off and on. I'd say the last two years of his life they were there all the time. Dr. Nick made sure they were there. They lived in a trailer out behind the house. They were in and out. Trish Henley and her husband had a trailer out behind the house. They were back and forth up there. The medication problem was getting so bad that they needed somebody there. Elvis had trouble. He was an insomniac. He didn't sleep. That's what killed him. He took sedatives and antihistamines on an empty stomach, and he died. It killed him.

Q. Is it true that on his final night he took all his medicine packets?

A. He took them all at once that night, because he couldn't go to sleep. So he took every load. He took all four packets — Attack 1, 2, 3 and 4. He took all of them. He took all four of them. And he had an empty stomach. Elvis was the type person that if he had to lose 50 pounds before a tour, he'd try to lose it the day before he left. So, he hit the floor and died. Just OD'd for the last time. I'm sure when you overdose nobody sets out to do it, but he did. So that's what happened.

Q. Did Elvis consider himself an addict?

A. Elvis never considered himself an addict because he had doctors. Why would he? He never got anything off the street. He would take his Demerol shots and his Dilaudid shots in his hip and stuff like that. It wasn't illegal drugs. It was all legal. He put prescriptions in everybody's names. That's why he was able to get the massive amounts.

Q. Is it true that Elvis wanted to buy a drugstore in downtown Memphis?

A. Tried to. He just never got around to doing it.

Q. Do you believe Elvis' final overdose was a form of suicide?

A. No. I mean, anybody that does that to themself eventually kills themself. But Elvis didn't say, "Well, I'm going to do it." No, that didn't happen.

Q. Did he ever attempt suicide in any way?

A. No, never.

Q. Did he overdose more regularly as the years went by?

A. Uh-huh. Like I said, the last year of his life was the scariest thing in the world. Just constant emergencies all the time.

Q. Would the ambulance come up to the house?

A. No, not the ambulance. It never got that far. That would be in public records. You can't do that. When Elvis would go into the hospital with some sort of ailment, he was put in the hospital to dry out. That's the reason he was there. No other reason. I mean, he'd had some problems with his liver and stuff like that. But Dr. Nick put him in there to dry him out. That's why he was there. It was always some other story.

Q. Did Elvis' personality change as he got deeper into drugs?

A. You could watch him change. The pills disguised everything. You couldn't tell if he was up or down, because he'd be messed up. You didn't know. When Elvis was straight, there wasn't a better person in the world. But when he'd get messed up, you didn't know what he was going to do. He'd get mean as a snake.

Q. Would he break things?

A. Oh, yeah, sure. He wouldn't throw things at you. He'd just break stuff. He'd knock stuff around, bang it around, stuff like that.

Q. Did he have a fear of shaking hands?

A. No, didn't bother him.

Q. Did Elvis have a cleanliness fetish?

A. No.

Q. Did Elvis have a decorating scheme for Graceland?

A. Elvis liked things that were ornate, you know. He didn't like antiques, because he said, "I grew up in antiques. Why would I want to go buy 'em?" Elvis would go shopping for furniture in Memphis. He'd walk in and say, "I want that, that, that" and leave. Never even ask the prices.

Q. Did Elvis set up an actual recording studio in Graceland?

A. We did a session there. We did it out in what they call the Jungle Room. We called it the den.

Q. Did the house change after he passed away?

A. No, the house pretty well stayed the way it was.

Q. Did Priscilla re-do the house?

A. No, she kept it intact.

Q. Did Graceland have a staff of cooks 24 hours a day?

A. Yes. They didn't live on the premises. they'd come back and forth. Had a nightshift, dayshift, three eight-hour shifts for all the time. Somebody was there all the time.

Q. Is it true that Elvis and you guys would jump on the jet and go to special places to buy some food and then come right back?

A. I caused that problem. We didn't have anything to do one day. I said, "Let's go get a sandwich in Denver." He said, "Where?" I said, "There's a great place there that's got peanut-butter-and-jelly sandwiches." So he said, "Fine. Let's do it." We all did. $40,000 round trip. But that's the mythology of that. I created that myth. I'm the one. It was my idea. He decided, "Let's go do it."

Of course there were other times when Elvis would jump on the plane to go anywhere. He'd say he'd go out to Las Vegas to get, say, some of his diet food and stuff like that, but he'd go out there to get some of his medicine he needed. That airplane was like a car to him. You just drive it somewhere. He had two jets. Sometimes we'd be about 10 or 15 of us on the big jet. On the small jet, all you could hold was eight people. Colonel would use the JetStar, and Elvis would use the 880. If one of us had to run back and get something, we'd take the JetStar. Run back and get it, stuff like that.

Q. The plane and the pilot were on call 24 hours?

A. Well, not 24 hours. We had to adjust it. Elvis, had he had his way, he'd have had it 24 hours a day, but he couldn't. I told him, I said, "You can't do that." To set the plane up for take off took at least an hour. Now the JetStar, you go out there and refuel, you were gone, but that 880 was an airliner. You had to go out there, you had to cater that plane, refuel it, get the crew onboard. I mean, it took about an hour to get that plane ready. Elvis would want that plane immediately. The small jet, we'd jump on and just hop anywhere. A lot of times we'd take it to Las Vegas or wherever we wanted to.

If "instant gratification" were described in a dictionary, Elvis' picture would be beside it. Everything was just instantaneous, a headlong rush to get it done before he died. I don't think that Elvis — deep down in the recesses of his consciousness — ever thought he'd live a long time anyway on account of the short-lived part of his family.

Q. Did Elvis fly alone?

A. Not on his private plane, no, huh-uh. Never went by himself on that. I was with him on that.

Q. Was a peanut butter-and-banana sandwich Elvis' favorite food?

A. That was just one of the sandwiches Elvis ate. He would eat something until he didn't like it anymore and wouldn't eat it again. He would just get tired of it. Like cars, people, anything. He got tired of it, that was the end of it. You never saw it again. In '56-'57, Elvis would eat mashed potatoes and gravy and sauerkraut and very crisp-fried bacon and sliced tomatoes. And he ate it so long and so often that he got tired of it. He quit it when we got back from Europe. I remember that's all he would eat for lunch. Then sometimes he'd have a hamburger. He ate a lot of pork, more pork than he did beef. That's the way it was in the South back then.

Q. Was Elvis not a fan of ribs?

A. No, he wasn't. Elvis liked hamburgers and ham and bacon and stuff like that. He wasn't a bit fond of ribs. Elvis didn't like to eat anything with his fingers. It bothered him. If you ever licked your fingers, he'd tell you to leave the table.

Q. Did you observe any drastic change in his habits the last year of his life?

A. The last year of his life, one of the telegraph messages that I got when I saw him do it — because it telegraphed to me what was going on — Elvis started back eating sauerkraut and mashed potatoes and gravy and bacon and sliced tomatoes … what he'd eaten in the late '50s. It was like he was trying to get back to a simpler, more innocent time.

* * *

~ The Inner Elvis:

Feelings, Emotions, Sorrows & Joys ~

- "There's got to be a reason why I was chosen to be Elvis Presley."
  — *Elvis Presley to his hair stylist, Larry Geller, April 30, 1964*

- "The image is one thing and the human being is another … it's very hard to live up to an image."
  — *Elvis Presley at his pre-show press conference, Madison Square Garden, June 9, 1972*

Q. Would you say that, overall, Elvis was a happy person?

A. At the beginning, he was, sure. Very happy. I mean, he was a kid. He had all this stuff going on. Enormous amounts of money. It was like hitting the lottery. He was doing the whole thing, and he enjoyed it. Yeah, it was fun. It was a lot of fun, in fact. Meet every star you'd ever grown up with.

Q. Do you think he ever seriously contemplated a change of career?

A. No — never, ever. Elvis did exactly what he wanted to do. He wanted to be an artist, and he got to be one. He never wanted to be anything but that. What he did was what he wanted to do. There was nothing else he wanted to do, period. In fact, he never even talked about what he would have done if he wasn't doing music. I don't think he thought his career would last the length it did. But you know, he told me once, "If it stops, I'll be happy. I've done everything I wanted to do."

Q. Early in his career, was he worried by the intense debate about whether his music was immoral?

A. No. Elvis went with the flow. He thought it was funny. It never really rattled him that bad. He couldn't understand what all the rigmarole was about, but he knew what he was doing at all times. Elvis was never in his life ever not aware of what he was doing or who he was. He knew what he was and knew what he was doing. He was a gunslinger, and he knew how to shoot. That was his thing. He knew it. It wasn't a case of him not knowing what was going on, because he knew what was going on.

Q. Was Elvis obsessed with his public image?

A. Elvis never knew at any given time what caused whatever he did. It just happened. I remember one time Wolfman Jack was backstage. Jack asked Elvis, "What's it like to be Elvis Presley?" Elvis just stopped cold. I was sitting right beside him. He said, "Where did that question come from?" I said, "I have no idea. Can you answer it?" He said, "I don't think I can." He finally told Jack, he said, "I can't answer that. I don't know."

That was probably the best question I've ever heard asked of Elvis, and he couldn't answer it. He just said, "I don't know. I don't know what it's like to be me. I don't know what you're talking about." It just stunned him. It was like somebody had landed in a flying saucer and started talking. He just didn't know what to do. It never hit him what he was, or how he was, or what caused it. He said, "What the hell kind of question is that? 'What's it like to be Elvis?' I don't know." He didn't know.

People forget that Elvis started in this business when he was 19 years old. He literally grew up in this business, so he didn't know anything else. He wasn't trained to be a performer or a movie star. He didn't know about it. Elvis didn't know anything about anything. Elvis used to sit down and ask me questions. He'd say about some experience, "What is that like?" I would say, "Just like this," and explain it to him. He didn't know. He just did not know.

Q. Was Elvis in awe of other celebrities?

A. He didn't know who anybody was. Important people would walk up to him, and he would be completely unaware of their celebrity. Once in 1957, Henry Kaiser came up to me and said, "I want to meet Elvis." I said, "Elvis, I've got somebody who wants to meet you. It's Henry Kaiser." He said, "What does he do?" And he was dead serious. There was nothing phony about that statement. I said, "Elvis, are you kidding?" He said, "No. Tell me."

I said, "Well, the biggest steel company in the world is run by Henry Kaiser and Jay Kaiser. He built this hotel we're staying in, the Rainbow." Back then it was a Kaiser hotel, not the Rainbow Hilton it is now. I said, "Elvis, he's probably one of the greatest industrialists that ever lived. He built the Liberty boats."

He said, "What are they?"

I said, "They are boats that everybody rode across the sea in during World War II." This was 1957. He didn't know. And he said, "Fine. I'll meet him." He shook hands with Kaiser, said, "How you doing?", talked a few minutes, and that was the end of it.

Mr. Kaiser later on would come out to the beach and sit down and talk to us. He said, "That's the strangest guy I've ever met. It seemed like he didn't know who I was." I said, "Mr. Kaiser, he has no idea who you are."

Elvis was never out in the world. He graduated from high school in 1953, got a job, and a year later was making records that changed the world. He didn't know who anybody was. It's not that he didn't care. He just didn't know. He hadn't had time to develop that part of his basic knowledge.

Q. Would he depend on you to keep him updated?

A. Elvis depended on Joe Esposito or myself to orient him about people. You know how when you meet someone whose name you can't remember, so you have them introduce themselves to a person standing next to you so they'll say their name? Elvis would do that.

One night in Las Vegas, Arnold Palmer was backstage before the show. As we moved through the room, I would run interference. I said, "King center, you've got such-and-such, such-and-such, such-and-such. King to our left, you've got such-and-such. King to our right, you've got Arnold Palmer."

Elvis said, "Lamar, who is that?" I said, "Elvis, he's probably the greatest golfer that ever lived." He said, "Oh, really?" And I said, "Yeah."

He said, "Well, what does he do?" I said, "Introduce him as the Babe Ruth of golf." And he said, "Really?" I said, "Yeah." He said, "Okay."

So onstage Elvis announced to the crowd, "I'd like you to meet the Babe Ruth of baseball."

I mean, nothing ever registered. He just did not know who Arnold Palmer was. Elvis never read the paper. These big industrialists would walk up to him, and Elvis didn't know who they were. He just never cared. He lived in his world, and he moved his world around with him. That's what it was.

He depended on me more than anybody to tell him who these people were. Like these big directors would come up. I knew who they were. I'd say, "This is such-and-such." He'd say, "Oh, okay." And he would tell them some of the pictures he had seen, because I had told him. They thought it was Elvis saying it.

Elvis had never seen these guys' movies. He didn't know what they did. He could care less. But he loved movies. He loved stuff. It was that simple.

Q. It's true, then, that Elvis lived completely in his own world?

A. He had a commitment to his world. Elvis was not what everybody thought he was. Elvis was what everybody wanted him to be. He was himself. I mean, he had his own personality, but it's like God put His hand on Elvis' head and said, "Here's where you are."

106

I've compared Elvis to a guided missile. He was put out there to do one thing. And that's what he turned out to be — a superstar. Nothing was ever planned. We didn't know from one minute to the next what was going to happen with his career. It started and got bigger and bigger and bigger.

He and I would just look at each other, and I'd say, "What's next?" He'd say, "I don't know." He didn't know. He had no idea. He knew who he was, but he didn't know.

Q. Truth or myth: Elvis was afraid of his public but also desperately wanted them?

A. That's what his whole being was about, being who he was. Stars wear sunglasses like they don't want to be seen. But they wear sunglasses because they want to be seen. People tell you that they're in it for the art. Stars love the recognition and the money and the fame. Who are they trying to kid? You know they like it.

There's nothing wrong with that. I think it's great. I like to be somewhere and a guy walks up to me, "You're Lamar Fike." I say, "Yeah." I love that. That's great. I'm not so self-effacing that I don't think that it's abnormal. I can be some place and somebody will walk up and say, "I know you. How are you doing, Lamar?" and the whole thing. Well, that's from recognition, but it's reflected glory any way you look at. Still, that's what people do. That's what they strive for.

Q. Did Elvis try hard to please his public?

A. That's always the thing with an entertainer. They always want to please somebody. That's what makes them entertainers. They want to do it. Don't forget that when Elvis made that demo for Sam, it was for his mother. Went and paid $2.00 to have it made. That was for his mother. He wanted to be an artist. He always wanted to do it, but he didn't think it'd take off like that. All of a sudden, it did.

Elvis was not a goer and doer. He didn't like to go to premieres. He didn't like to go to parties. He just didn't like to do it. He was a lone wolf. He was an only child, and he didn't have a lot of friends. Even until the day he died, Elvis didn't have a lot of friends. The friends Elvis had were us. He had nobody else as friends. He didn't trust anybody. Nobody got to know Elvis. Very few people got to know Elvis. He didn't want them around him. He didn't like them. So he had us around him, and he understood us.

Q. Was Elvis a prisoner of his own fame?

A. Elvis was never a prisoner. Understand, Elvis could have gotten out and gone anywhere at anytime he wanted to. It was up to Elvis. If he wanted to get out, we could have covered it, and we could have done it. You have to understand. You've got to want to do it to do it. He didn't want to do it.

He wouldn't hang out that often. At the last, he wouldn't hang out at all. He'd go out on his own. Sometimes we'd have to corner him, because he would try to get in fights and stuff, because he was so messed up. Somebody would pop off to him. Elvis would get ready to whip his ass, if he'd be high.

But Elvis was never a prisoner. That term is just awful. He never was. He could have gone anywhere and done anything he wanted to at any time. He chose not to. It was his choice, not ours.

Q. Did Elvis like being famous?

A. He was happy being a rock 'n' roll superstar. He loved it. Elvis loved being a superstar. He thought it was great. He liked all that attention and crowds and starting riots and stuff. He loved all that. He thought it was great. It was kind of like having a job.

Q. Would you describe Elvis as a humble person?

A. He was humble, and he liked to stay humble. He played that role. But around us, he'd get meaner than a snake. People never saw that. We were the buffer zone. Sinatra didn't have that buffer zone around him. Elvis did. Had Sinatra had the buffer zone around him that Elvis did, a lot of stuff that got out about Sinatra would never have gotten out.

Q. Would you say he was a down-to-earth person?

A. He could relate to people. That was Elvis' thing.

Q. Was Elvis a shy person outside of the limelight?

A. He was a very shy person. Elvis was very shy.

Q. Even with the success that he had?

A. He was very shy, very shy. People never knew that. And yet he appeared in public as a very confident person. A lot of bravado. That's why the drugs and stuff. See, it made him a little more brave and courageous. But Elvis basically was a very shy, quiet person.

Q. Did he get out into nature much?

A. Sometimes he would go out but very seldom. Elvis didn't like the outdoors. He didn't like it that much. He just didn't like it. He didn't like the great American outdoors. It wasn't one of his things.

Q. Was Elvis' horseback riding phase due to Priscilla's influence?

A. No. He liked to do that. He'd go out and ride every once in a while. Elvis got over things real quick. He'd get onto something, and then he'd get off of it. He liked the ranch, because he had fun at the ranch, because he had a lot of borders around it and nobody could get to him, so he liked the ranch to go and get away. He liked that. That was a lot of fun. Put up that big, high, wooden fence. Nobody could see in. But he couldn't put it all the way around it, and that bugged him. He enjoyed that, the solitude of it, where he didn't have people bugging him.

Q. Was he a materialistic person? Did things matter to him a lot?

A. Not really, not in a greedy, acquisitive way. Elvis was bored. He could have anything he wanted to. If not, he could put one hell of a down payment on it. That's just the way it was. He'd go out and buy 24, 25 cars in one day. It'd drive Vernon crazy. Scared Vernon half to death. Never bothered Elvis. Just the way it was. He'd like those cars, and then he might give them away.

Q. Was Elvis a regular churchgoer?

A. He was never a regular churchgoer. He was brought up Assembly of God, AG. He'd have a minister come by or something like that. He would see them every once in a while. He was never that into that. He liked Rex Humbard. But not that many other ministers. Elvis was religious in his own way.

Q. Do you think Elvis could have become a televangelist?

A. He could have been anything he wanted to be. Elvis was a leader. He just never had the guts enough to do it. He had guts enough to do what he did, not anything else. Elvis was non-confrontational. He did not like change. Elvis was a singer and an actor. Nothing else. He didn't want to be anything else. He didn't want to try it. He just did not like change. It was one of his things. Elvis never went out of his comfort zone. I wish he had. He'd probably still be alive. But he never did.

Q. Was there one special thing in life that gave Elvis the most pleasure?

A. No. It was just whatever. He liked going out riding in cars. We'd go out and ride around, stuff like that. We'd go out on a boat, something like that. He loved getting on his private plane and flying places. He enjoyed that. We'd go up to Aspen and Snowmass Village. We actually stayed in Snowmass. We'd get out there and ride on the snowmobile. He loved stuff like that. That was fun. And all of us together playing Monopoly and games. Just all staying at the house together. He liked that.

Q. Aside from his mother's death, was there anything that gave him unbelievable grief and pain?

A. When he caught Priscilla being unfaithful.

Q. With his fame and wealth, was Elvis still what you'd call "a common man"?

A. He was. He was a very normal person, I think would be the term. He was as normal as he could be under the circumstances, which were pretty wild. The regular guy, whether he'd be out picking cotton or working a job, could relate to Elvis. That was part of his fame.

Q. Is it possible Elvis suffered from bipolar disorder?

A. We think so. If anybody in the world showed bipolar-type symptoms, he did. Elvis was manic. There was no doubt about it. He'd go up and down in a second. Then he'd crash. He'd be high, and then he'd crash.

Q. Did this contribute to his drug use?

A. I think Elvis' drugs were to hide his being shy. That's the way he made himself comfortable around people. There's so much psychological tick to what Elvis did. You can't literally say it. But he just liked drugs. I mean, it wouldn't have changed his way around anybody. He just liked them. There weren't no ifs, ands, buts about it. He loved them.

Q. Did he keep a diary of any kind?

A. No. Elvis at times would be by himself and would write stuff down. But I've never heard him make a statement like that in my life. Never heard that. No diary has ever been found.

Q. Did he write letters to people?

A. Yeah, a few. He wrote one to George Klein. He wrote one to Alan Fortas. Wrote one to a girl there in Memphis. He wrote about four or five letters, but he would write down notes and stuff. He made notes on all of his book liners and everything. When he'd memorize a song, he'd write the song down so he could memorize it. That way if it came straight from his hand to the paper, he could remember it better, so he would do that.

Q. Was astrology one of Elvis' hobbies?

A. Yeah, he liked it. He thought there was a whole mystic thing out there. He was into that *Cheiro's Book of Numbers*. He got into all kinds of mystical beliefs. Elvis believed in divine providence. He believed that he was put here for a reason. We read books on it and stuff. We had a guy that came with us awhile, Larry Geller, who got Elvis into all that mystic stuff. That's what really messed his head up worse than anything — all that mystic shit Larry Geller got him into. It got kind of difficult there.

Q. Did Elvis' interest in the occult influence him in a significant way?

A. No. He liked it, but he didn't let it influence him. He was just fascinated with it. Color charts. He liked color charts and colors and symbolism.

Q. Was Elvis good at karate?

A. He was good. Elvis was a good, honest third- to fourth-degree black belt. The whole crew was taking karate. My arthritis that I've got today is from breaking bricks and boards and stuff. My hands are screwed up to this day from arthritis from breaking stuff. Back then, you don't think anything is going to ever happen. Later on, it does.

Q. Did he actively play racquetball?

A. Racquetball, nah. Everybody else played racquetball. Elvis stood there, let the ball come towards him. He wasn't into exercise. Karate, he would do that. But as far as handball, racquetball, no. He bought that racquetball court and everything. Elvis would go out there. You'd hit the ball and if it came toward him, he'd hit it. If not, he wouldn't touch it. He wouldn't move.

Q. Would you describe Elvis as fundamentally a lonely man?

A. He sure wasn't alone! He had us around all the time. He would get up there in his room because he liked to be alone. It wasn't any big mystcry about that to us. Elvis was lonely, but I mean, he was lonely of his own accord, not of what somebody perceived him to be. But he didn't do anything to change the perception. That was his thing. He'd get up there in his room with his girl and stay up there four or five weeks. If he wanted to be around anybody, he'd come down and be around us.

Q. Did Elvis ever say he would not want to be who he was?

A. No, I never heard Elvis say that. Elvis always loved being Elvis. Loved it!

* * *

~ Living on the Edge:
Elvis and Danger ~

- April 5, 1936: an infant Elvis survives a tornado that killed 235 people and destroyed the church and houses across the street from the Presley residence.

- May 13, 1955: 14,000 fans at an Elvis concert in Jacksonville, Florida, storm the stage in an attempt to touch him, provoking a riot, his first.

- February 18, 1973: four men jump onstage as Elvis performs in Las Vegas; Elvis knocks one down with a karate blow and suspects they may have been sent by Priscilla's new romantic interest, Mike Stone, to embarrass him.

- June 24, 1977: near Madison, Wisconsin, Elvis sees an altercation between a gas station attendant and two youths; he leaps out of the car, confronts the combatants and gets them to cease fighting and shake hands.

- At the time of his death, it is estimated Elvis owned 39 guns; in 1970 alone, he spent $19,792 on guns (*Las Vegas Review Journal*).

Q. Was Elvis attracted to danger? Dangerous people, dangerous situations?

A. Yeah. But he was never scared of it. It just never worried him. He just wasn't scared of a lot of stuff I can think of. He was never, ever frightened about stuff. No, I can't think of anything he was scared of.

Q. Except maybe his health?

A. That bothered him, but he didn't realize how bad it was, so he wasn't scared.

Q. Do you think he was a hypochondriac?

A. Yeah, I'd say Elvis was a hypochondriac to a degree. Elvis liked medicine. When he was young, he would chew aspirins. He'd open a thing of Bayer Aspirin and eat the whole thing, because he liked the taste of that, what they did for him, stuff like that. That's why he got into the Physicians' Desk Reference, the PDR. He'd find something wrong with him. He'd go to his PDR, and that's the medication he'd get from the doctor, because he knew how to tell them what was wrong.

But the biggest fear Elvis had in his life was his voice. If something went wrong with his voice, he'd go crazy. That was his big fear. He would go out of his mind. It would scare him to death, if he started getting any inkling of any kind of problem. Elvis had his tonsils in his mouth until he died. His tonsils had holes in them and stuff. He never would take them out. He was scared it would change his voice.

Q. Did his tonsils cause him frequent pain?

A. Oh, yeah. He'd be two or three days where he couldn't talk. Scared him to death. He'd go bananas. He wouldn't take his tonsils out, so he always thought something was going to take his voice away from him. Doctors recommended a lot of times he take them out. He wouldn't take them out. They stayed in his mouth, and they were in bad shape. The doctors said they had holes and everything else in them. He just wouldn't take them out.

Q. Was he ever seriously threatened by any person or particular type of person?

A. Crazy people. There's no other way to put it. Crazy people. But that's the element you have even today. Everybody's going to do that. But the element with him was a little stronger. That's why we all carried weapons. Elvis didn't wander out a lot. He'd rather have done something with us or get a girl up there or something like that. He didn't care about roaming around in public.

Q. Were you ever aware of a foreign power trying to use him in some political way?

A. During his Army days, he once mistakenly went across the line into East Germany. He got lost and got back on the other side real fast, so that there wasn't any problem. But, no, no foreign power ever tried to manipulate him for any purpose. They didn't know what to do with him either.

Q. Was Elvis ever subjected to a credible terrorist threat?

A. Terrorism was never really there the whole time that Elvis was alive. Elvis died in 1977, so, I mean, terrorists were not a big thing then. There were always threats on his life. That was a continual thing. People always did that. That's the reason we were all armed.

Q. Did he have any serious stalkers?

A. Yeah, we had stalkers, but we didn't know what they were. Back then we never heard the term "stalker". Somebody would hang around the gate a lot, I guess it would be a stalker. We had stalkers. We didn't know they were stalkers. Everywhere we'd go, they'd be there. But we didn't know what they were. We'd just say, "Well there's so-and-so again…"

Q. In the early days, was Elvis very accessible to the public?

A. No, he wasn't accessible. Elvis was never accessible. Certain people at the gate, when he'd come out the gate, he'd sign autographs, stuff like that. But he was never accessible. The problem people had with Elvis all his life, and the reason I guess why there's hundreds of books written about Elvis, is he was never accessible. Nobody ever knew what he did. They didn't know. I mean, the gates of Graceland would close, and then it was our life. I mean, everybody stayed on the other side of the fence. We'd get behind the gate. That was the end of it. Nobody knew what we did. The great escape.

Q. Did the FBI ever keep him under surveillance?

A. The FBI had a continuous surveillance on him. Hoover didn't trust him. Hoover had a dossier on Elvis thicker than that damn TV set. You can get the FBI files on Elvis. They are there. Elvis never knew it. It was later on we found out about it. But a lot of times when these guys threatened to kill him, these shooters, the FBI guys would come by. You know, talk to us and stuff.

Q. Did anyone ever seriously try to blackmail Elvis?

A. They always tried that, be it some way or another. "You're this" or "You're that". We'd stop that real fast. It never got out of the infancy stage, you know. Back then, you didn't have the electronic media like you've got now, so we were able to control publicity better. We could literally control it.

The latter part of Elvis' life, we couldn't. It was getting out of hand. It was not good at all. The early part of the career, you could pretty well control it, because they didn't have the paparazzi and stuff like that. They could never get to him. We were called the Memphis Mafia for a reason. We were a mafia. We kept everything at a distance. Nobody knew what was going on. We kept it out. It didn't leak. When it did, that was not good. But as a rule, we kept a pretty tight ring around him.

Q. Did the Italian Mafia or organized crime ever approach Elvis or try to infiltrate his operation?

A. They approached through Colonel in the late 1950s, early '60s. They tried to get him early on, but Colonel wouldn't let it happen. Even when Elvis was in Las Vegas, the mob was kept out.

Q. What explains Elvis' intense interest in law enforcement during the 1970s?

A. He was always fascinated with uniforms. He liked the Army from the standpoint of wearing a uniform and all that stuff. He loved that. The discipline bothered him big time, but he liked the idea of it. Elvis was never on an entry level on anything. It had to be at the top. Elvis, when he went into something, it had to be at the top. So when he wanted to be recognized as a law enforcement agent, he went to see President Nixon. Couldn't get more top than that.

Q. Did Elvis carry a gun with him all the time?

A. As a rule, yeah. Started really in the 1960s after we came back from Europe. It became more prevalent in the 1970s when he was heavy into drugs and stuff like that. Elvis always carried two or three guns on him.

Q. Did he really shoot out televisions when displeased with the program?

A. Yeah, he really did.

Q. Was that a regular occurrence?

A. Uh-huh. He just didn't like what was on the television, so to turn it off, he'd just blow it out. That way he didn't have to get up. If he didn't have the remote, didn't want to hunt for the remote, he'd just shoot it, you know. If this was at a hotel, we'd just take it and buy it, put it in the belly of the airplane and bring it back to Memphis and throw it away.

Q. Did he shoot them up in the house also?

A. No, not as a rule. Just when he was on the road.

Q. Did Elvis and the group often shoot guns at Graceland?

A. We would shoot at night. Nobody would be out there in the back. They had these big railroad ties that Vernon had set up, and we'd shoot into the railroad ties. Open the door up and shoot up into it like that.

Q. Is it true that secretaries in the office would hit the floor when the shooting started?

A. No, there was never anybody in the office when he shot off his guns.

Q. Would the police get phone calls from the neighbors about the shooting?

A. Uh-huh. They used to get a little uptight.

Q. Would the police come into the home or just to the gate?

A. Word was that somebody was at the gate — police were down there. So we'd just stop shooting. He was isolated there for a long time. At the end, everybody moved around him.

Q. Did Elvis ever shoot guns in the house?

A. Elvis would shoot whenever he felt like it. We'd duck under the table when he did.

Q. When arguments among you all got heated, would Elvis pull out a gun?

A. Yeah. At that house on Perugia Way in Bel Air, he took a .357 short-barrel and cocked it right in front of my face. I watched the shell come into the chamber. It was about an inch from my nose. We were arguing. I was winning the argument. He said, "I'm going to stop the argument." He did.

Q. Did Jerry Lee Lewis go to Graceland with a gun one night?

A. I was there. It was in the 1970s. He was in his Rolls Royce in the driveway, and he kept hitting the gate. He was drunk. I was in the next bedroom when Elvis called me and said, "I want you to see something." And I came back over into his bedroom. He had three cameras set up that observed everything on the property. About five screens. He said, "Just look down there." I said, "What is it?" He said, "Jerry Lee trying to get in."

Elvis never liked Jerry Lee. Never got along with him. He just didn't particularly care for him. I said, "What are you going to do?" He said, "I'm going to call the police." Elvis got on the phone, called the police, said, "Get down here and get this son of a bitch at the gate right now." He had him arrested.

Q. Did Elvis own a submachine gun?

A. He came down to a recording session with a submachine gun in his hand one time to scare everybody to death, and it did. It was a real Thompson submachine gun. But the equipment wasn't broken or shot up. He just did that as a practical joke.

Q. Where would he get a Thompson submachine gun?

A. Probably from somebody in Chicago. Probably through the mob. Could be anything, you know.

Q. Did Elvis ever talk about life after death?

A. Elvis believed in a very strong afterlife. He thought that's where it was. It's like the old axiom: everybody wants to go to heaven, but don't nobody want to die. He was a very strong believer in God and everything, because he was brought up that way — Assembly of God — and life was real simple with him. It was: you die, you go to heaven. If you took care of yourself, that's where you went. I'm quite sure Elvis went straight there. He had no reason not to.

Q. What were Elvis' thoughts on organized religion?

A. With Elvis, the matter of religion was cut and dried. Elvis delved into a lot of different religions, and he was interested in them and read about them. They tried to get him one time into Scientology. He wouldn't do that, either. Elvis knew where he was going. He knew what he wanted. He believed in an afterlife. He believed that his mother was there, and he believed he was going, too, so there was no doubt in his mind.

Q. Did he ever hold séances to talk to deceased relatives?

A. Elvis never had a séance. No, he never did that. That's something he never got into. I don't know why he didn't, but he didn't. He never tried to contact anybody in the afterlife. No, he never did that, never, ever.

Q. Did Elvis believe he had supernatural powers?

A. Yeah, uh-huh. He would get into Daya Mata, the Mormon lady who became a Hindu, and different things like that. He thought he could heal. Somebody would have a headache. He'd put his hand on their hand and say, "You got a headache anymore?" Well, they wouldn't say, "Yeah." They'd say, "No, I don't have it anymore." He'd thought he healed them.

One time I had a big sinus headache. He said, "I'll heal that." I said, "Okay." He put his hand on my head and he says, "It's gone, isn't it?" I said, "No, it's hurting worse."

One day, we were driving, and he pulled up, and there was a puddle. Elvis was going through a period where he thought he could heal people. I said to him, "Heck, Elvis, don't worry about that puddle. You can walk on water." And he got real mad.

* * *

~ __Elvis Is in the Building: The 1970s__ ~

- January 14, 1973: a live television concert, *Elvis: Aloha from Hawaii*, is seen worldwide by an estimated one billion people in 40 countries.

- From his performance at the International Hotel on July 31, 1969, to his final concert at Indianapolis' Market Square Arena on June 26, 1977, Elvis gave 1,137 live shows — an average of one show every two-and-a-half days.

- In the mid-1970s, scalpers were able to charge $500 a ticket for an Elvis concert at the Las Vegas Hilton.

- Between 1970-1977, 34 albums of Elvis' music were released, the same number released from 1956-1969.

Q. The *'68 Comeback Special* led to Elvis returning to regular live performing?

A. That's what put him back on the road. We flew into Vegas, and Elvis and I got off the plane and got in a car with Colonel. Colonel said, "You know, what you did on the show we can do in Vegas." Elvis looked around at me and said, "Well, I can tell you what's getting ready to happen." I said, "What?" He said, "We're getting ready to do Vegas." He was right. Colonel was setting it up. He was letting Elvis know by talking about something else what was going to happen.

Q. Was it Elvis' idea to start touring again in the late 1960s?

A. He was tired of the movies. He was worn out with them. The movies were all such formula pictures. He didn't like them. Colonel knew he had to do something to get Elvis' activity level up. So we started going back on the road, and that got his activity level back up. Then he started playing Vegas.

He just hated the pictures. He just didn't want to do them, because Colonel had signed all these notoriously bad deals. Elvis had to play them out and he didn't like it. So as a consequence, we started playing Vegas and touring. He liked that for a while.

Q. After not touring for so long, how did Elvis adjust to playing Las Vegas?

A. Right off the bat in Vegas, he didn't like playing four solid weeks at a time. No musical performer has done that before or since. I can't think of anybody that's ever done it since, that's played there for four weeks. Elvis' show was a hard show anyway. You'd do it twice a night for four solid weeks. Maybe a week of it, but not four straight weeks. It was hard on us. It was hard on everybody, including him. I think Vegas speeded his death up more than anybody did. That's when he got heavy. The heavier he got into drugs was always in Vegas. To keep going, he would load up.

Q. What was the audience capacity at that time for an Elvis show in Vegas?

A. He pulled 2,200 people in every show. With two shows, he put in four to five thousand. Nobody has ever beaten the record before or since.

Q. And his fee was a basic guarantee?

A. $125,000 a week.

Q. No percentage of the gate?

A. No, and it was not a good deal. He did it until he just couldn't do it anymore.

Q. Was Elvis overwhelmed by the demands of the performing schedule?

A. It was just hard. It was just hard to do it. You're cranking up four shows, sometimes three shows a night, and it's difficult. That's hard work. It's demanding. Vegas itself is not easy, because of the desert air and stuff like that. Vegas is a tough town. People who play Vegas now go in there and play three or four days, maybe a week. That's it, and they're out. But not going for four straight weeks. We'd go in there for two weeks before, and it'd take us two weeks to unwind afterwards. So we're basically in Vegas mode eight weeks.

Q. Was a special venue ever built just for Elvis?

A. Just before he died, the Hilton Hotel built an enormous room for Elvis. It was not built for anything else but him. The plan was for Elvis to do one show a night. He'd done a two-hour show, and that'd been the end of it. He'd put in 5,000 people in there, 10,000, and that'd been it. That was the reason that room was built. He hated doing two shows. Couldn't stand it. Hated it! If he'd gone to the big room, he'd have done one show a night. But he died. They built that room for him to do that, and he died. So they turned it into fights and stuff like that, but that room was built for him. There was nobody else.

Q. Did Elvis have any special performance rituals or superstitions?

A. No. Before hitting the stage he'd warm up and sing and play the piano. Something like that. He'd drink hot tea and honey with lemon in it.

Q. Did you harmonize with him on songs before a show to help him warm up?

A. Oh, we'd always do that. We'd go out and sing. Ride in a car and sing like that. I'd do the lead line and he'd do the harmony. I can't hear harmony. He could. So I'd sing a lead, and he'd do the harmony to it. We used to do that in Europe and everywhere. We did it on the piano. He loved to do that. But there wasn't any ritual.

Q. The myth of Elvis smashing a guitar before he came on every night is not true?

A. I never heard of it in my life.

Q. Did the Colonel hire the band?

A. No. Elvis would do it. But the Colonel would set up the deal. Our first band that we hired, the reason we hired James Burton was because I liked James Burton. Ricky Nelson was a friend of mine, and I always liked James' picking. And I told Elvis, "We need to get a guy named James Burton." He said, "Can you get him?" I tracked that deal down. That's how it started to come about. It sort of left-handed went with me and about three or four others. Elvis literally built his own band. He was influential, and word went out. He paid those guys a lot of money. God, I mean a lot of money.

Q. Did they rehearse a long time before the tour?

A. Not really. He'd go out on tour. Boom, he's gone. He's out. That was it. Elvis never rehearsed a show at the site. He would rehearse before the tour. They'd go in and work a little bit, but he'd never do sound checks. He just went out and did a show. Like when we went to Las Vegas, we didn't even know how to light the show, he and I. Elvis said, "How are we going to light this son of a bitch?"

I had learned a fair amount about lighting from a guy named Hugo Granada, who used to light Dinah Shore. Hugo was probably one of the greatest light men that ever lived. Hugo taught me a lot about lighting when I was with Brenda Lee, when I managed Brenda for a year. I just took it forward with me, and so I set up Elvis' light show when we came to Vegas. Elvis and I did it together. Did the same thing with his show lineup. It was all off the top of his head. Nothing was really planned with Elvis. Not a thing I can remember.

Q. How large was the touring ensemble?

A. He basically carried an orchestra with him. Joe Guercio had the orchestra. They would carry about five or six more pieces with them. He'd have his band, maybe six, seven more pieces. Had some brass pieces with him. But they would be pickup bands. Joe would carry a nucleus out and then build the band around them. All told, it built up to 73 people on the road that we were traveling with.

Q. How did the group travel?

A. We loaded everybody on buses. We had three aircraft and two tractor trailers with the lights, and we'd take a whole floor of the hotel. They'd take a floor below us. We'd take the other floor. They were never integrated in with us. Never, ever.

Q. Was Elvis punctual?

A. Always on time. We were there with him, so it was just we were on time. We were there. We had to be there. So we didn't have any problems with that. We were there. We just had to do it, which is what it was.

Q. What wardrobe did Elvis travel with?

A. He took 30 suits with him in those big anvil cases. He had his whole wardrobe to pick out what he wanted to wear. Elvis never packed. Elvis' bedroom was moved. His jet was a flying bedroom. Elvis went from one bedroom to the other to the stage to his bed. His jet was a flying bedroom. He had a king-sized bed. He had a master suite in the back of his jet.

Same thing when he'd get at the hotel. He'd have a big master suite there, presidential suite. We would scotch tape the windows to keep sunlight from coming in. He didn't want it. He didn't want the light coming in so he could sleep. We carried loads of aluminum foil, just loads of it, and scotch tape. He created his own portable nest.

Q. Even when he played near Memphis, did he also stay in hotels?

A. When we played Memphis, he wouldn't stay at the house. He would stay at the Rivermont Hotel up there on the river. Because he didn't want to stay at the house. He said, "I feel like I'm at home." He never wanted to play his hometown. He hated it. Once again, we had run out of venues.

Q. Where did Elvis get the ideas for the extravagant outfits he wore during the 1970s?

A. Elvis got the cape and the Taking Care of Business-TCB idea from Captain Marvel. The lightening bolt was Captain Marvel. That's where Elvis got it. People don't realize where he got this stuff. We grew up on comic books and Superman and Captain Marvel. That's where he got it. TCB was, he just liked the idea of taking care of business. He designed the thing symbol. The lightening bolt at one time was supposedly the West Coast symbol of the Italian Mafia, so that's how it all came about.

Tender Loving Care, TLC, he gave to the girls. Even had designs made up, drew them up and the whole thing. The concept and the actual wording was from him. People laugh at some of these things. They think they're extravagances or something. But you look at that and you just say, that man had an enormous amount of creativity that spun off and filtered off in different directions. It's like his mind really never stopped.

Q. Did he ever think the Nudie suit was a little over-the-top?

A. He wore it one time for an album cover, and he'd wear the jacket. He never wore the full suit on stage because it was too hot. He'd wear the jacket. The jacket was leather. He'd wear that. But he wouldn't wear the full suit, no. It was just too gaudy. He hated it.

The custom suits that developed with the high collar, he designed himself. He liked the high collars. You see all these old actors, like Gable and Lancaster, always did it. They turned their back collar up because of their necks, so their necks wouldn't be geeky looking. So Elvis would turn his collar up. Sinatra, all of them, wore these big collars, you know, that curved out like that. That was all to hide your neck.

Q. And the capes?

A. That was Elvis' idea, too. He liked capes. For 23 years, almost a quarter century, Elvis had this non-stop fulcrum of creativity. All the time. It was unbelievable.

Q. Did Elvis come up with the "Space Odyssey" introduction?

A. He came up with that. He always loved the theme from *2001: A Space Odyssey*. In fact, we didn't even know what it was. We thought it was the theme from *2001*, and the actress Jill St. John, she's married to Bob Wagner, she came backstage after we'd opened up. It was about the second or third night we'd opened. She said, "Whose idea was it to do *Thus Spake Zarathustra*?" I said, "I never heard of that song. Where did it come from?"

She said, "That's the theme he does at the beginning. From the symphony by Richard Strauss." I didn't know it was from that. I thought it was just the theme from *2001*. I told Elvis. He said, "No shit!" I said, "Yeah."

Q. Who came up with the close of the show?

A. The theme song, we came up with that. We were upstairs, and he said, "How am I going to close this?" I got to thinking. I said, "Let me think about it." So about an hour later, I said, "You know what, Elvis? Everybody likes *I Can't Help Falling in Love with You*."

He said, "That is a great idea. Why not? I'm glad I thought of that."

I said, "I'm glad you did, too." And I said, "Make that just your closing song." So that became his signature closing song.

Elvis' show had a tremendous amount of dynamics in it. Elvis loved dynamics. Big, powerful endings and stuff. He loved all that. Joe Guercio used to call him Elvis the Brass Killer. He'd just wear a trumpet out. Just wear them out. Their lips would fall off.

Q. Did Elvis play the guitar on the shows?

A. He played. Elvis strummed the guitar. He knew about seven or eight chords. That's all he knew. I play the guitar today, and I sound just like him, because he taught me how to play it. I know six or seven chords. My cousin Tommy McDonald said, "You hear Lamar play and you hear Elvis." I learned how to strum. He taught me how to do it in Germany. That's it. Elvis could chord on the piano and stuff like that. He could play on the guitar and do the chords.

Q. Did Elvis ever do any private shows?

A. No, never. No. No. No. Elvis never did that. No, absolutely not. No way. No corporate work, no birthday parties. Back then, nobody did it. That whole period of the 1960s, there was really no live performance for him at all. It was just straight movies. Elvis didn't do steady live performing for almost 12 years.

Q. Did Elvis go to the Oscars, the Grammys, any of the big music or movie award shows?

A. No. The Colonel used to get mad at the Oscars, because all these people are going there for nothing. The networks charge all that money to do it, and none of the stars got paid anything. Colonel hated that. He couldn't stand it. He said, "I don't want Elvis to go to any of those." And Elvis never went to any award shows because Colonel didn't want him to. Otherwise, Elvis had to be paid to be anywhere. That's the way it ought to be, when you think about it. At one point he appeared at a Jaycees function. They were awarding him some type of award, "Young Man of the Year". The Colonel was very mad at that, because it was a way for them to draw crowds and not pay Elvis. Colonel hated awards.

Q. Did Elvis like touring?

A. He liked it at first, but he didn't at the end. He got to hating it, because he got tired of going back to the same places. He just detested it. You don't know how much he disliked it. It got so old and so boring. That's what I said about the apathy. One year we played Monroe, Louisiana, three times. How many times can you do it? We played in little towns like Kingsport, Tennessee, and over there in Arkansas.

Elvis would say, "What are we playing these things for?" Because we ran out of venues. Colonel wouldn't let 'em in. I mean, there were like 40-50 offers every day coming in for Elvis to tour outside the United States. I mean, it was unbelievable! It was scary. Had we gone into Brazil in '72-'73, Elvis would have drawn 200,000 people. I mean, he'd walk on stage to a set of people he'd have had flipped out. This was what he needed. He needed to recharge the batteries. You can't keep doing the same road every day.

Q. How was the Colonel able to keep these offers at bay?

A. The Colonel would raise the price up. He wouldn't say no. He'd raise the price up. But he couldn't go out of the country, so he couldn't control the situation if he wasn't with Elvis. As a consequence, we didn't tour, and it was not good. You can't keep doing that. He did, and consequently, Elvis just gave in. He got tired. He was in it for the money towards the last.

Had he gone to Europe, we would have started off a tour in England and gone and played four or five days in England, and then gone into Germany and played another 10 days in Germany, gone to Spain and played another five or 10 days in Spain … gone to Denmark, Holland, Belgium, you know, it would have been Russia, everything.

Q. Did Elvis read his concert or record reviews?

A. He would read the bad reviews and get pissed off about them. They put him down big time. We'd just try to keep everything away from him. Any good press was bad press to Elvis. He'd pick out something the guy said. It'd piss him off. So he just got so he didn't read it. He wouldn't read his reviews. We just wouldn't put his reviews around him. They'd talk about his weight and stuff like that. He'd go crazy. Just get mad and start throwing shit, make our life miserable.

Q. Did he change his repertoire on the road?

A. He changed it all the time. He would put new songs in but not that often. *Funny How Time Slips Away* by Willie Nelson. He liked that.

Q. Were his performances at the end truly listless or without spirit?

A. Toward the end when he got real tired, they were that way. You know, you can't do his type of performance two or three times a night. Nobody holds up under that. He didn't. He took everything to try to keep going. It was really not good. He gave so much in his performances. At the end, he was just so fed up and tired. In Vegas, for example, it was a bad contract. He was being paid $125,000 a week. That's a lot of money, but it's not worth that.

Q. Did his fans protest when he gave a weak performance?

A. No. The fans accepted him. Any way they could get him, they accepted him. Had they got up and walked out on him, I think he'd have shaped up even better, but they accepted him any way they could get him. When you're that big, it all becomes what they'll put up with, I guess. Elvis would forget lyrics. We'd keep the lyric sheets on stage with him, so he could read them. It happened a lot of times. That's from the drugs.

Q. Did a concert ever get cancelled because of Elvis' drug illness or emotional problems?

A. He would just get so screwed up. Like the time we canceled out in Baton Rouge, Louisiana. It was because he got mad at Ginger, so he decided he wanted to go home. He just said, "That's it. I'm going home." Well, when you do that, you can't be responsible for lawsuits and stuff like that, so you put him in the hospital immediately so you can get out of the lawsuit. You do that with any entertainer. There's nothing unusual about that. That's been going on forever. You have to. If not, you're going to face the lawsuits. As it was, nobody turned their tickets back in. Nobody got their money back. Everybody kept their ticket. And then, they wanted the souvenir.

Q. Did you ever have a lawsuit from a promoter?

A. No, because they hoped he was coming back. He did makeup shows. He did it in Louisiana, in Baton Rouge. Yeah, we went back and did makeups. Several of them.

Q. How burnt-out on touring was Elvis at the end?

A. The last year, year-and-a-half of his life, he was miserable. He couldn't confront Colonel with it, and he wanted to go out of the country, so he just was not happy. He was not a happy person at all. He hated tours because it was the same old places, going back again. They ran out of venues. It took a big venue to hold Elvis. I mean, Elvis got real excited when we played Madison Square Garden, because that was different. He hadn't played New York since he did the *Ed Sullivan Show*. That was different.

Had we toured Europe, he would have been really ready to go. He would have been ripping and roaring. He'd have been ready. He was bored! It's called apathy. If he'd have gone to Europe, he would have sold out.

We played Houston one time, and he got back on the bus, walked by me, and said, "Where were we?" I said, "You were in Houston." He didn't know. To any entertainer, be it Elvis or anybody else, there's an airplane, a limousine, a service elevator into the room, limousine into the venue, sing the venue, get back in the limousine, go back to the hotel, go back to the plane, you're out. They don't know where they are. They could care less. How are you going to know in those circumstances where you are, unless you ask somebody?

As a rule, he didn't give a shit. He didn't care. When he was messed up, he really didn't care. It was very rudimentary. He'd go on autopilot and just start singing.

Q. Was it tough for Elvis to decompress after a show?

A. He wanted to be by himself, but he wanted the people around, the people that were closest to him. He'd be really down for a while, because, you know, you have that adrenaline rush and you'd stop. So you've got to unwind. He hated unwinding between shows. Used to drive him crazy.

He would come downstairs and would hang out in his dressing room and order something up light to eat or something like that. He wouldn't eat until about 2:00 or 3:00 in the morning normally.

He'd eat a couple of cheeseburgers before he went to bed, you know, and stuff like that. He'd choke on it sometimes. You had to watch that.

Q. Would he talk about the performance?

A. Sometimes he'd talk. Very seldom. He'd come in and say, "Let me ask you this question" or something like that. He'd say, "Lamar, I don't like that the way that light hit me." I'd say, "Well, let's change it." We'd talk. We'd critique the show. That's why he hated doing two shows, because you've got to go down and come back up again. That's why on the road you do one show, you're out of there. He hated Vegas, because he had to do two and three shows in a row. He hated it! He hated getting back up, and he hated going up and down. Sometimes we'd do three shows a night. He hated that.

Q. When did the phrase "Elvis has left the building" start?

A. It was always there. We used the line in 1957 when we'd be on tour. Al Dvorin, who was with the Colonel and did all the merchandising, said it to keep the fans from rushing Elvis. If we were at a stadium, he would say, "Elvis has left the stadium." When we got in a building, he said, "Elvis has left the building." There was nothing really magical about that statement. It was a true statement. They did that to let you know that he wasn't in the thing, don't try to come backstage, don't rush the stage, don't try to get back. He's already left the building. He's gone. And that's how it came about.

Now it's turned into a great American phrase. Frasier Crane uses it on that show, "Frasier has left the building." Everybody uses it. Now it's just a standing running joke, but there was nothing magical about that phrase. It was just to let people know he wasn't there and not bother hanging around. He was gone.

* * *

~ <u>Nearing the End</u> ~

- July 19, 1977: a Los Angeles radio psychic predicts Elvis will die soon.

- August 1, 1977: the critical exposé book *Elvis: What Happened?* is released, infuriating Elvis.

- August 8, 1977: Elvis throws an all-night party for Lisa Marie at a local amusement park.

- August 10, 1977: Elvis weighs an estimated 260 pounds, begins a new diet to prepare for upcoming New England tour.

Q. What was it like being with Elvis the last year of his life?

A. It was horrible. Probably one of the worst years of my life. Number one, to see your friend dying in front of you. And number two, that you can't stop him. And number three, he don't want to be stopped. So, you know, you have to do as best as you can. That's why we were blamed for his death. We couldn't do anything about it.

If Elvis would get mad at you, he'd fire you. Well, if you're fired, you can't do anything for him. If you're not there, you can't help it. You had to waltz this ring. You had to do this very strange dance. It was the dance of death. You had to really literally do everything you could to try to keep him alive. But I mean, you know, if you weren't there, you couldn't do anything at all.

In my life, I don't believe I've ever had anything scare me or frighten me or make me more uncomfortable than that last year of his life. It was like living on a razorblade. It was just that scary. It was just absolutely frightening. You were scared to breathe.

We'd do these shows, and he'd be so messed up that he couldn't — it was like a nightmare that never went away. With the intensity of those problems that went on, there was no way for this guy to live. I mean, just, you couldn't put yourself, your body through what he put himself through. Just impossible.

Q. So you and his other close friends had to maintain an illusion of normalcy?

A. We put up with a lot to try to help him. As far as I'm concerned, everybody has said this. Probably, if it hadn't been for us, Elvis would have been dead five years before he died. I mean, we kept him alive probably five more years. If it hadn't been for us, I know of five, six, seven, eight, or nine instances he would have died. I'm talking about dying. He swallowed a peach pit one time. Joe had to pull it out of his throat. It went down his throat. It lodged in his throat. He was dying. Joe pulled it out of his mouth. Happened in Las Vegas.

Q. Were there other times you had to intervene to save Elvis?

A. He would start OD-ing, and we'd bring him back around. That's the reason Dr. Nick was there every day — to keep the guy from dying. I've seen Dr. Nick give him a shot of Ritalin straight into his neck to keep him alive. This guy was in horrendous shape. The worst I've ever seen anybody. I don't think I've ever seen anybody before or since in as bad a shape as he was in. Unbelievable. It was horrible.

When we would travel, we tried to have a doctor there all the time. We had to. If we'd go on a tour without a doctor, it was scary. We'd find out where doctors were to get him in there as quick as we could, because you never knew if he was going to make it. We didn't know if he was going to be alive the next morning. It was like being a fireman and the fires never went out. It's the only way I can think to say it. We didn't sleep.

Q. Did Dr. Nick contribute to his death?

A. Dr. Nick did contribute. I mean, Elvis owned doctors. People use doctors. Elvis bought them. He literally paid for them. A lot of things Dr. Nick could have done that he didn't do, but that's beside the point. Everybody gets caught up in everything. Dr. Nick got caught up in everything. It was a lot to get caught up in. You get caught up in that whole lifestyle. Dr. Nick could have not done it, but he didn't choose to.

I mean, we're all responsible for our own actions. You can blame anybody you want to, but ultimately anything that goes wrong, I mean, you take responsibility for your own actions. If they ever build another statue in the harbor of New York, it ought to be a Statue of Responsibility to Your Own Actions.

And the last person that Elvis ever blamed was himself. No star ever blames himself. It's everybody else, not him. If they go down the tubes, it's everybody else's fault, not theirs.

Q. Was Elvis' last year a sort of slow suicide?

A. No, it wasn't a slow suicide. I just knew it was going to happen. I didn't know when.

Q. Was there ever a time you saw him unconscious and thought he was dead?

A. I remember one time in Houston we put Elvis in a bath of ice water. We went down and emptied two of those big ice machines and put ice in the water. Put in a tub full of ice to wake him up. He was so messed up. Dr. Ghanem, myself and Joe had him in the tub full of ice water. Nothing but ice in the water, to bring him back around. God, it was scary!

Q. Did he go into convulsions?

A. No, he just wouldn't come out of it.

Q. Did you ever think Elvis would grow old gracefully?

A. I just never could see Elvis old. I never could see it. There was no way. You don't live in that intense light that he was under for as long as he did. They are lucky that he lived as long as he lived. People are very lucky that they got him as long as they did. There's nobody before or since that lived under the intensity that he lived. Name me one. There ain't. There was no let up. Never let up. It started and never stopped. I was with him for 23 years. I never saw it let up.

Q. Can you recall the last time you spoke with Elvis?

A. Before I left for the tour, I had gone down to Memphis and was there with him a couple of days before. We'd talked and hung out at the house. At that point I traveled on the advance team with the Colonel, because I just got tired of fighting Elvis. I couldn't win. And we'd get on the road, I'd see Elvis, and he'd say, "You're okay?" I'd say, "I'm fine, but you're not. You're messed up."

It got really bad. We fought all the time. Elvis was trying to figure out a way to get rid of me, and he couldn't. He told a couple of the guys he was going to fire me, but he never did, because I would confront him all the time with it. And it got so bad and so pervasive that I didn't want to be around it. So in order to keep from him and I confronting each other, I would go out with the Colonel. Colonel always stayed a day ahead of Elvis.

For that last tour, Colonel requested me because Elvis had fired Red and Sonny. I mean, Vernon fired them. Colonel needed one of Elvis' guys with him. Colonel and I got on the road. We'd fight all the time. Colonel would start arguing with me. I said, "You don't order me around." We fought. Colonel and I fought all the time.

Q. Is it true that, at the end, Elvis believed he could make changes in his career, his lifestyle?

A. No, he didn't. There was no plan to change things. That was the problem. He had nothing to look forward to. He wanted to go to Europe, but Colonel would never do it. It became such a burden. He wouldn't confront Colonel about it.

As a consequence, Colonel just kept on doing his same old way. Elvis should have toured Europe. He should have toured Europe starting in the early 1970s. 1971 or '72 is when he should have toured, but Colonel wouldn't set it up. So it became burdensome.

Toward the end, Elvis was fighting Colonel about this and about Colonel's gambling. Elvis would use something else to get rid of some other problem. And Colonel's gambling and everything like that, that brought it up.

The underlying problem was that Elvis was confined. He couldn't get out of the country, and it pissed him off. He hadn't done anything to deserve staying like this. He said, "They want to see me. This is where I need to be." But he would just sort of — it got back to that non-confrontational situation. He wouldn't do it.

Q. At the end, do you think Elvis was consumed with depression?

A. Depression, yes, I think so. If Elvis died of anything, he died of terminal apathy. He felt there was nothing else to conquer. Nothing else to do. I think Elvis would still be alive had we toured Europe. He wanted to go out of the country. How many times can you do Monroe, Louisiana, and Shreveport and these places? Colonel kept going over and over again and kept doing these. And Elvis got tired of it. He said, "I need to go somewhere else." And he got so apathetic at the end that he didn't care anymore.

What bothered Elvis was the apathy of it. He wanted to go other places, and he felt hemmed in. The reason he got mad at the Colonel was because he couldn't face trying to get out of the deal, and he would get mad about other stuff.

I think that last year of his life was so frustrating, because he couldn't get out and do what he wanted to do. He wanted to go to Europe. He wanted to tour Europe. Hell, he had been there in the Army. He liked it over there. They loved him over there.

Had we done a tour, I think he'd still be alive. He'd have lasted another 10 or 15 years, I think. I don't know. I think that it would have helped him, because it was a challenge. Something different.

The only thing different left in Elvis' life was to tour the world outside of the United States. And the Colonel wouldn't let him do it. It was just horrible the Colonel did that, but that was the way it was.

Q. Do you think Elvis would have met the rigors of a world tour?

A. Anytime he had a great challenge in front of him, he'd always meet it. He would have got his weight down. He'd have dried up. He'd have got himself straight. He'd have gone to eating like he did back in the early 1970s. He'd have been that good-looking in Europe. He'd have looked like the star that everybody thought he was. That's the way he'd have hit there. But he never did. Never got the chance. Had he done that, that would have extended his life. How long? I don't know, but it would have extended his life longer than it did, if we'd have gone around the world. He wanted to tour around the world. That's why he bought that 880. He wanted to use that aircraft to go everywhere.

Q. Beside stalling the promoters with high fees, what other excuses would the Colonel use?

A. Colonel kept telling him, "You got security problems over there." You know, Elvis believed it. I said, "Elvis, we need to get out of here." And he wanted to do it, but he just wouldn't go up against Colonel. Right toward the last, Elvis was ready to do it, because he needed the money. If we'd have done a worldwide tour, Elvis back in the 1970s would have made probably 50-60 million dollars.

Q. Why did the Colonel have to go along on a non-U.S. tour?

A. Colonel was a control person. He couldn't have his artist out of his sight. The Hawaiian special, for example, was in the United States. That wasn't out of the country. It was across the water, but it wasn't out of the United States. Colonel set that up. He did that. That was his deal. He set the deal up with the guy at RCA. First time a satellite thing had ever been done. We did it at 11:00 at night, so it could go around the world, on account of the time zone difference. The response from that was phenomenal. It brought the sales up on the records, on the movies, everything. That showed what kind of market was out there for a world tour. Had we toured Asia, it would have been phenomenal. He could still be working outside the United States. He could have been like Sinatra doing worldwide tours and stuff. They couldn't get enough of him.

Q. Near the end, did Elvis like playing Memphis?

A. He never wanted to play his hometown. He hated it. Once again, we run out of venues. He was just tired. He was worn out. He was bored. Apathy causes a lot of stuff. That's when his drug habit got him, because he'd zone himself out. He was so miserable.

Q. Do you blame that on Colonel Parker's unwillingness to set up international tours?

A. I blame that on Colonel. I don't blame it on anybody else. I blame Vegas on Colonel. I blame a lot of things on Colonel. I think Colonel did more in the latter part of Elvis' years to hurt him than he ever did to help him.

Q. Do you think it was intentional?

A. No, the Colonel was just full of fear. Elvis was the only artist he had. Oh, he saw it. Just ignored it. I told him. We all told him. Colonel ignored it. Colonel owed debts. He'd get Elvis back in there to pay some of his gambling debts down. He didn't give a shit about Elvis.

Q. Earlier that final year, Elvis fired much of his staff, including some longtime members of his inner circle; was it because of money problems?

A. That's not true. Elvis had an influx of money that was always there. I don't think Elvis would ever have gone bankrupt. He could make money like an Arab oil sheik when he went out and worked. The reason everybody was let go and we quit and stuff like that was because, man, nobody could put up with it. It was just hell. That last year was a rough year.

He couldn't risk running out of money. You've got to understand that Elvis spent money like it was going out of season at sundown. I mean, it took a lot of money for Elvis to operate. Running Graceland alone probably cost him $40,000-$50,000 a month. He ran two aircraft. He ran an 880, which is seven feet shorter than a 707. He ran a Lockheed JetStar, another four-engine jet. And they were all in his name. He didn't have a corporation. Everything was in his name. Elvis spent money. So he had to work. It wasn't a case of not.

See, Elvis was non-confrontational. He could not confront anything. I mean, Elvis would have loved to live in a world without red lights. He just couldn't confront anything. He just didn't know how to do it. So he would let somebody else do his dirty work.

He let Red and Sonny go that way. We flew into Palm Springs. When we got to Palm Springs, I said, "Where's Red and Sonny?" Elvis said, "Daddy fired them." I said, "What do you mean, 'Daddy fired them'?" He said, "Well, Daddy … and I okayed it." I said, "Well, you should have not done that. You should have told them yourself."

Q. Did Elvis consider taking time off from touring to regain his health?

A. Right before the last tour started we were talking. I said, "You know, Elvis, why don't we just take a year off."

He said, "You know, Lamar, I've been thinking about that."

I said, "Well, why don't we do it? Let's take a year off. Let's go to Hawaii."

There were no Betty Ford clinics back then. There was no such thing as a Betty Ford Clinic. There was nothing set up to do anything like that.

I said, "Let's just go over there and get rid of all this shit. Let's clean our act up."

And he said, "Lamar, I'm not going to have you do that. I won't be able to pay everybody."

I said, "There's two or three of us will go over there with you for nothing." And I would have. I said, "I'll stay with you."

He said, "Lamar, when we get back off this tour, let's talk about that."

That was in his mind, but he died before he started the tour.

* * *

~ **The Final Day** ~

- **August 15, 1977, 12: 28 a.m.** Elvis is last photographed by a fan as he drives into Graceland.

  10:30 p.m. Elvis visits a dentist, has two teeth filled...

- **August 16, 12:00 a.m. midnight.** Elvis returns to Graceland to prepare for his August 17 concert in Portland, Maine.

  4:00 a.m. Elvis plays a game of racquetball with cousin Billy Smith...

  4:30 a.m. Elvis plays the piano, his last songs, *Blue Eyes Crying in the Rain* and *Unchained Melody*...

  5:00 a.m. Elvis goes to bed, takes first of four packets of pills...

  9:00 a.m. "I won't." Elvis' last words, spoken to Ginger Alden, who warns him not to fall asleep in the bathroom...

  2:00 p.m. Ginger awakes, discovers Elvis lying on bathroom floor, calls for aid...

  3:30 p.m. Elvis is pronounced dead at Baptist Memorial Hospital.

Q. When did you last talk to Elvis?

A. I talked to him about 20 hours before he died. I called him on the phone. He answered the phone. He had a hotline beside his bed, a red phone. Two or three of us had the phone number. If we wanted to talk to him directly, didn't want to go through anybody, we just called him on the red phone.

I said, "How you doing?" He said, "Well, you know, my eye hurts." Because he had a secondary glaucoma. And I said, "How are you feeling?"

He said, "Lamar, I don't feel like doing this tour." I said, "Well, just cancel it."

He said, "Lamar, you just can't."

I said, "Why can't you? Who said you can't?"

"Well, I never thought about that."

"Just cancel it and let's go. Let's just get away. Let's take a year off. Let's not do anything."

He said, "Lamar, I've got a payroll to meet."

And I said, "Elvis, I know that. But there's a lot of us that'll stay here and work with you. I will and probably some more of the guys would."

He said, "Lamar, let's get through this tour. Let's talk about it then."

I said, "Okay. Just get yourself well."

He said, "Okay, but I don't feel worth a shit today. I feel bad."

And I said, "I know it. You're overweight. You don't feel good."

He said, "Well, you're the only person in the world can get away with saying that."

I said, "Well, you know I'm right."

And he said, "When we get off, let's talk about that."

I said, "Fine."

Didn't happen. He died the next day.

Q. When you were in Portland, Maine, preparing for the upcoming concert and you heard that Elvis had died, did you think it was a hoax or publicity stunt?

A. No. I knew it was true. I just knew it. It wasn't a case of not knowing it. I knew it. I'm the one that kept saying it was going to happen. I was not surprised. I was in shock because I had just left him. It's like somebody dying of cancer. When they die, it still shocks you. That's what it was. It's just really, just once again, the stopping. Everything came to a screeching halt. You have to understand that I was with him for 23 years. All of a sudden, I lost him. It was just devastating. You don't get over that easy.

But you know, no matter what anybody says or does or talks out there, and all these experts that know him, you know what? I was with him. They weren't. So I mean, you know, the part is, I've done it and did it, and been there, done that, even bought the t-shirt. So I don't know. You take it like it is. You never think that anybody is going to die. But with him, I thought he was. I just didn't know when. It was just one of those bad situations.

Q. Do you think Elvis had any idea he was going to die that suddenly?

A. I don't think Elvis had any inkling he was going to die. His mother's side of the family was so short-lived that, you know, the indications were all there. The way he was doing everything. You just can't keep going like that. Nobody can keep going like that.

Q. He didn't show any unreasonable fear or concern about a sudden death?

A. Can I tell you something? Nobody thinks they're going to die. Nobody wants it. Just like I said, everybody wants to go to heaven, but don't nobody want to die. That's the premise. As far as an inkling, no. I think that somewhere in the back of his mind he knew, but you put it so far back that it never comes up. You just shuffle it way back there. But I think that moment when he started OD-ing and he hit the floor, he knew what was going on.

But you're so messed up, you don't care. He had bitten almost through his tongue. Dr. Elias Ghanem was with me. When I flew in, Elias met me there. In fact, Elias and I had a room together at the Howard Johnson. Elias said, "Lamar, I can tell you. When you bite through your tongue like that, you're choking to death. You are suffocating." And Elvis was in his rug. He was in that big, shag rug and he was suffocating. That's exactly what it was. That's why he bit through his tongue. He was fighting to get his breath. He was so messed up he couldn't roll over. When they found him, he was on his knees with his face in the floor. That's the way he died. Not good.

Q. What did you do when you heard the news?

A. I flew back to Memphis that day. I went over to the funeral home. They had me go over and check the body. It was laying there under that sheet. Wasn't a pleasant sight. It was Elvis. There's nobody else. It was Elvis. But he just looked horrible. People said, "Well, he didn't look good." Well, my God, his face was all mashed in. They had to redo his nose and everything. His whole face. Post-mortem lividity had already set in. He was a dark blue. That's from the blood pooling. That's how you find out how long somebody has been dead.

Q. What was your first thought when you saw him in the funeral home?

A. I was mad at him.

Q. Who determined the pall bearers?

A. Vernon did it; he picked them out. I was one of them. Had me on the side. My cousin, Tommy McDonald, called me yesterday and reminded me that our friend Kenny Davis of The Mountain Smoke Band was telling him about the coffin coming from Oklahoma City. I hadn't known that. Tommy said it was copper and silver, and that's why it was so heavy. And that coffin had been in that place in Oklahoma City since about 1952-53. That casket back then cost $30,000 in 1977. Money today, it would be what? $150,000-200,000.

The casket was so heavy that it almost killed us. Like I said, when I picked the casket up, I said, "God, man, he tried to kill us when he was alive. He's trying to kill us when he's dead." I mean, that casket was heavy. I was one of the pall bearers. I know. It was horrible.

Q. Was there a controversy about Elvis' will?

A. Yeah. Elvis revised the will two or three times right before he died. The original will was never found. Let me put it that way.

Q. Did anyone dispute the probate?

A. We left it alone. I mean, Elvis had left me quite a bit of money. Something for the rest of my life. So I don't know. You know, there was a lot of stuff going on. That's one of the sort of unanswered questions.

Q. So when Elvis died, Vernon got control of the estate?

A. Well, naturally, it fell into his hands. And then after he died, it went to Lisa. When Vernon started getting sick, that's when he appointed Priscilla legal guardian for Lisa, so she could control everything. She got a percentage of the estate.

Q. Do you think Priscilla has competently managed the estate?

A. She got in there with a good group of advisors, and they built the estate back up. It was a bad situation. I think she did quite a bit to help it, and I think that the advisors did, too.

* * *

~ Elvis Lives: The King's Legacy ~

- According to the Harris Poll® of August 12, 2002, one of four Americans (25%) remember where they were, who they were with, or what they were doing when they heard that Elvis had died.

- Graceland is visited by more than 600,000 people in an average year … an average of four people call Graceland each day and ask to speak to Elvis Presley … according to Elvis Presley Enterprises, Inc. (the official estate of Elvis), the total economic impact on the city of Memphis from Graceland visitors is estimated at between $300-400 million per year.

- There are more than 600 Elvis fan clubs worldwide, an estimated 35,000 Elvis impersonators worldwide and an internet search with the words "Elvis Presley" will yield 29,600,000 results.

- According to Harper's Index®, 13 countries have issued at least one Elvis Presley postage stamp, 189 U.S. state and federal court opinions written since 1977 have included a reference to Elvis and the three best-known Western names in China are Jesus Christ, Richard Nixon and Elvis.

Q. What is it about Elvis' life that makes some people regard him as almost a saint or a divine being?

A. It's absolutely true. There is a Church of the Living Elvis. It's in Colorado. It's the great American dream, isn't it? Elvis was from a very poor upbringing, and he loved his mother. It's like mom and apple pie. He became a very successful superstar and made a lot of money. He had a tremendous amount of respect for his mother. He said "yes, ma'am" and "no ma'am" to people. He was very polite. He was very quiet — except around us he was another person.

That's what everybody liked. He was the epitome of Southern elegance. He really was respectful of his elders and stuff like that. He was the epitome of a Southern boy who made good. And he was unearthly good looking. He was just extremely good looking.

Q. Do you think Elvis grasped the significance of his role in revolutionizing music around the world?

A. He didn't know he was a pioneer, but that's the way it was. He had no idea. Elvis really was the founder of rock 'n' roll. Elvis brought mainstream rock 'n' roll to the white people. John Lennon said it better than anybody. He said, "Elvis opened the door. We just ran through it." That's what he did. Everybody out there today that's in rock 'n' roll owes their career to Elvis.

He was a nova exploding off of the old star and becoming thousands of times brighter than the original, and the brightness lights up everything around. He was a child of destiny, regardless of whether he wanted it or not. At times he really didn't want it.

Q. Is Elvis' ongoing popularity due only to active merchandising, or do you think more people have discovered and learned to respect his music?

A. I think it's all the above. People have had more time to reflect now. I think the estate has done a pretty good job. They've done a very good job of keeping his name out there. So I think that it is all the things combined. Rock 'n' roll is just now getting so where it really starts respecting its past. And I think that's got a lot to do with it. You've got to look at the past to see the future, anyway.

Q. Are you surprised when you realized the surge of commercial popularity his music still retains?

A. Well, you know, they say, "Elvis made more money dead than he did alive." I say, "Had he been alive, he wouldn't be making it, because he was spending it. He's not here to spend it." The estate made 35 million last year. That's a lot of money. There are acts out there now that don't make anywhere near that. They work all the time. He's been dead.

Q. Has Elvis' music been accorded more respect after his death?

A. From a pioneering perspective, I think so. The only thing I can compare Elvis with, if you use any sort of analogy, is that it's kind of like Aborigine cave drawings. People take their children in to see the cave drawings. It's a generational thing with Elvis. People who liked him, their kids like him. It's generational. His timing was always so good that even he died at the right time, to be honest with you.

Q. Had he not died so young, how do you think his career might have developed?

A. I think that Elvis in another couple or three years would have been in a decline that would have been unbelievable. But you know, he would have gotten bigger in movies, I think, if he'd have gotten out of his shell. But he died, and then all of a sudden he got bigger. I mean, Elvis literally saved RCA Records. RCA was going to close down. When Elvis died, they couldn't print records fast enough. They had every plant going day and night. So he literally saved that label. Saved it. I mean, it was over with.

Sinatra went through a decline. Elvis would have gone through it, you know, where you don't sell there for a while, but he didn't go through it. When he died, Elvis was, really, declining big time. We were having trouble filling some of the rooms. Little subtle things were happening, and you saw them. Like I said, his timing was perfect. He got out at the right time. Hell of a way to get out, but he did.

Q. Do you think Elvis is regarded with more sympathy now that he's dead?

A. It's always easier to look back than look forward, isn't it? Because you look back, you got something to look at. Look forward, you can only imagine. So you can look back at generational situations and see how it changed history. History you can see. The future you can't.

Elvis became the ultimate music idol of our culture. I told Eric Clapton once, Elvis showed us all what could go wrong with rock stardom. He proved that drugs and money don't mix. He got so big, it was frightening.

People see what he went through — his childhood, his upbringing, how his character was born. The hostility that people showed him in his life, you're seeing that dissipate. But when you look back on Elvis' life, you see a lot more there. I don't think there's been an artist that's been so analyzed as Elvis has been.

Q. Are you surprised that his legend grows with each passing year?

A. He's an icon. Icons grow. They don't diminish. Graceland is the second most visited house after the White House. It's like the old newspaper axiom: "When the fact becomes a legend, print the legend." He did so much for the business. I mean, everything that everybody did later on was on account of him. That's just the way it is.

Q. Did he look at himself as a musical pioneer?

A. Elvis never thought of himself as a pioneer. He didn't understand the term. He just happened to be there. Elvis used to say, "There's room for everybody in this business." And there was. He used to tell artists that. He'd say, "Hey, don't worry about me. Worry about yourself."

Q. In 50 years, 100 years, do you think people will still be thrilled by his music?

A. Yes. He's an icon. They ran a thing on Biography taken from polls worldwide. Out of the top 100 people of the 20th century, Elvis was number 34, and he was just behind Albert Einstein.

Q. Do you believe Elvis' ghost haunts Graceland?

A. I'm sure his ghost is still there. When you die that shockingly, I think the ethereal body wanders around in shock. I think that sometimes it takes you longer to get to where you're going, but there is no time. I understand that after you're dead, time is nothing. There is no time. I mean, God doesn't have time. Time is a man-made object. God does not have time. I mean, he doesn't say, "Well, it's 9:00 Monday morning." I think sometimes a spirit is confused and stays where it is.

I think that when you die suddenly — plane crashes and things like that — I think the spirit rises, but it doesn't know where it's supposed to be. It's shock.

I've heard it said that sometimes when they see these ghosts in castles, these people are still there, and they don't understand why they're still there after 400-500 years, but 400-500 years is nothing, it's a drop of the hat.

I mean, there is no time. God doesn't go to sleep and get up. The time continuum, He invented. So I mean, earth, stars, everything, He put the whole universe in place. That's why the spirits have been wandering around. I mean, Elvis' ghost could be there. I don't know.

Q. Have you seen the tabloid exposés that claim Elvis is living in Europe?

A. Elvis is dead. The sightings started immediately. Certainly, sure. Oh, yeah. Well, nobody wanted to believe he was dead.

Q. Do you think his spirit is at peace now?

A. Oh, absolutely, certainly. Are you kidding? Man, he's in great shape. Nothing fazed him.

Q. Do you miss Elvis?

A. I still miss him. My god, I miss him every day of my life. It's something that goes on every day. Everything becomes more benign later on. The blunt edges go away. They get very smooth.

Q. After his death, what sort of adjustments did you need to make on a professional level?

A. The only fulltime trade I'd ever really learned was being with Elvis. I'm 66 now. Somebody says, "Act your age." I don't know how to do that. I was never taught to do that. I spent my most formative years with Elvis. Of course, over that time with him I learned a lot about presenting shows, about the entertainment business. I'd managed Brenda Lee and worked with Hill & Range publishers, chosen songs, helped produce recording sessions. But the suddenness of his death was so phenomenal that, I mean — our life surrounded him, and his life surrounded us. You live a life in a fishbowl, and whether it's vicarious or reality, you are there no matter what.

Q. How about on a personal level?

A. A psychologist explained to me, he said, "What you did is, when your father died in '54, you transferred that bond to Elvis." When I lost Elvis, it was going back to the first thing the second time. And it was really, it was just so detrimental. I still do things today that come from being with Elvis. I unconsciously do stuff. Somebody likes one of my watches, I'll take it off and give it to them.

Q. Do you have dreams where he seems as if he's still alive?

A. I've had them every day of my life since he passed. The intensity of 23 years with somebody is pretty strong.

Q. When Elvis talks to you in a dream, do you rehash past situations?

A. It's nothing where he comes back and sits down and says, "What do you think I would have done if I did this?" Nothing like that. It'll be an instance more like he and I arguing about all the drugs he was taking. Just things would happen. He would walk through my dreams somewhere. Something would happen, he'd be there. It was like he never died. In my dreams, Elvis is never dead.

Q. The moments in your dreams are just regular moments?

A. See, anybody else dreams about Elvis, it's some sort of ethereal moment. For me, it's not. He was every day of my life. Everything that Elvis did, I was with him. He was an integral part of my life.

I had a dream about him last night. We were talking about the car. I was going to have tires put on the car, and he said, "What do you think about those tires?" I said, "I don't know." And then I woke up, and he was dead. But right then, he's not dead. In my dreams, he's still alive. He's not dead.

I never say to him, "What are you doing here? You're dead." It's just like it's continued. It's not like he's dead. It's just like his death never, ever happened.

Q. What do you think you might have learned from all those years with Elvis?

A. Humility. Confidence. How to take what life throws at you and throw it right back.

* * *

~ Afterword: Why Elvis Matters ~

by L. E. McCullough

MY FIRST AWARENESS of Elvis Presley was the day I heard my mother say to her brother (my Uncle Larry Igoe): "With those sideburns, you look like Elvis."

That was 1956, and I was four years old. My uncle was a 25-year-old Philadelphian just discharged from the U.S. Navy. Hailing from an epicenter of urban doo-wop, he loved Elvis' rockabilly twang. And looked totally cool in sideburns.

As with so many others — then and now — it was not Elvis Presley's artistic output that first seized my attention.

It was his inherent, inimitable, inescapable Elvis-ness.

Elvis was not the first musician in history to engender widespread celebrity status and intense fan passion; the renown of 19th-century performers such as Jenny Lind, Niccolò Paganini, Jan Paderewski and Nellie Melba was greatly enhanced by interest in their personal lives (often stimulated by promoter/publicists such as P.T. Barnum in the case of Lind, or the food and cosmetic mass merchandising surrounding Melba).

The celebrity-burnishing process intensified during the 1930s and '40s as innumerable jazz and pop artists from Cab Calloway and Bing Crosby to Judy Garland and Frank Sinatra fused their musical artistry with unique personal "branding".

But Elvis was the first musician whose opinions about anything and everything (not only music) seemingly mattered to anyone and everyone at all times. His emergence as a performer coincided with the rise of television as a dominant and omnipresent mass medium shaping and steering the aesthetic tastes of millions around the globe.

Once you experienced Elvis in any format — record, radio, television, concert, film or even a photograph — your perception about the world and what could and might happen next was changed.

"I've compared Elvis to a guided missile," said Lamar Fike. "He was put out there to do one thing. And that's what he turned out to be — a superstar ... it started and got bigger and bigger and bigger."

To some commentators, Elvis was an accidental superstar; his fame, they maintain, resulted from randomly appearing at the right recording studio at the right time in American musical and social history, possessed of the right look, the right musical style, the right packaging.

As record producer Sam Phillips famously said long before meeting Elvis, "If I could find a white boy who could sing like a black man, I'd make a million dollars."

He found one in Elvis, and millions upon hundreds of millions of dollars were indeed generated once rock 'n' roll entered the commercial mainstream. But a visionary like Phillips could never have imagined the magnitude of cultural consequence his simple equation would unleash.

Because who — in a buttoned-down I Like Ike America — could ever truly imagine the phenomenon of an Elvis Presley?

Despite the influence of Sam Phillips, Colonel Parker and an army of record and film executives over the years, it was Elvis who ultimately forged his own identity and musical direction. He would always be the Elvis he wanted to be and nobody else.

His music integrated familiar strains heard in church and theater, on the jukebox, at a hayride singalong ... an ever-evolving mix of urban-rural, black-white, sacred-secular, folk-Tin Pan Alley idioms woven into the everyday soundtrack of Americans working, dancing, praying, partying, dreaming of the bright future they believed lay ahead.

Elvis channelled a diversity of musical voices in his head. His singular interpretation of those voices on his early Sun and RCA singles blew the cultural mind of 1950s' America and inspired a wave of musical contemporaries who created more synthesis and innovation, evoked yet more outrage and wonder, embarked upon ever-widening currents of exploration across the now limitless frontiers of pop music.

He went on to record more than 700 songs, a vast canon staggering in its variety that touched every point of the musical compass, from *Old Shep*, *America the Beautiful*, *Queenee Wahine's Papaya* and *Take My Hand, Precious Lord* to *Bossa Nova Baby*, *Cotton Candy Land*, *The Impossible Dream*, *Bridge Over Troubled Water*, *Santa Bring My Baby Back to Me* and adaptations of non-English numbers like *'Torna a' Surriento* (*Surrender*) and *Muss i denn* (*Wooden Heart*) along with a core of blues, folk and country standards.

Elvis didn't break the existing pop music mold. He created a completely new mold altogether.

The process began in his childhood, when Elvis relentlessly sought opportunities for creative expression in his economically humble, socially limited environment. Music allowed him to see beyond his isolated geographic milieu and expand his vision of personal self.

Like every other aspiring young performer, he spent years perfecting a hobby into a craft. He memorized hundreds of songs, spent thousands of hours listening to radio and records. He figured out tunes by ear on piano, plunked away at a cheap guitar, sang in his church choir.

For a decade before walking into Sam Phillips' studio, Elvis played in talent contests, at school assemblies, on local radio shows. He sang at nightclubs, took part in open mics and jam sessions, attended countless musical events and found ways to hang around successful musicians. He auditioned for groups and got turned down.

As he paid his musical dues, he refined his stage persona, putting significant thought into his clothing, hairstyle, performance moves.

On the surface, nothing different than any other teenager hoping for "a break".

Yet at some point during this apprenticeship phase, Elvis acquired that most elusive element critical to a performer's success — he learned how to make his listener care.

He sang from his heart. He sang to the hearts of his audience. His first demo recordings were made for his mother. Made from Love.

Even a song like *In the Ghetto* was not in Elvis' telling primarily a social commentary or political protest song … it was a song about Love. "And a baby cries." "And a mother cries."

Elvis' gospel repertoire represented a different kind of Love, and it was a repertoire he cherished until the very last hours of his life.

For Elvis, life was all about Love. Or the lack of it we all experience at some point in our days upon this earth.

By singing about Love — the deep, irrepressible, uncontrollable, unfathomable Love that can wound as well as heal — Elvis tore away pop music's bland façade with three-minute vinyl riptides showing us the turbulent range of emotions that are standard-issue with each and every human, emotions most of us are too inhibited to express without the encouragement and catharsis music provides.

To the very end, audiences came to see Elvis Presley because they had to.

They came to feel an excitement, a bond, a surging symphony of feelings as indescribable and overwhelming and as close to pure transcendent Love as you can get in a public gathering outside a house of worship.

For these last 60-plus years the music of Elvis Presley — and that of the millions of musicmakers of all genres following in his wake — has torn down barriers, brought people closer together, shown all who will listen how to open our hearts to ourselves and each other.

Because it's a better way to be.

And nearly four decades after Elvis left the building for good, it's still going on — all the barrier-downing, people-togethering, heart-opening — whenever music is heard anywhere on this planet.

That's why Elvis matters.

Today.

Tomorrow.

And as long as there is still a human voice somewhere in the universe singing the chorus to *Don't Be Cruel.*

* * *

Graffiti outside Graceland
(photo courtesy Harold F. Eggers, Jr.)

~ **Friends Recall Lamar Fike** ~

RAY BAKER: "I had a close relationship with Lamar. He could read me and what I was thinking about when we worked together in the music business. He and I did a lot of good things together. He liked to laugh, and he and I had a bunch of them together. My life is much richer in every way because our paths crossed. Never had a better friend in my life. Miss him a lot."

* * *

JIMMY BOWEN: "Lamar was just one of a kind. We always had great fun hanging out. We became good friends over a period of time, starting in the late 1950s in Hollywood. He was involved with Elvis, and I was involved with Frank Sinatra, Dean Martin, Sammy Davis and artists in that genre. Lamar and I shared a common trait of being people who grew up totally unprepared for such things. But there we were, at very young ages, right at the center.

"I always referred to Lamar as Elvis' Other Brother. Brothers fight, and brothers make up, and that was their relationship. Their world was so small, you're almost a prisoner of your fame. You're so isolated in that world, you'd better have a family around you.

"Lamar and I shared a belief that music is a mirror of the times. Those who are successful in music are very locked into that, whether they realize it or not. The times he and I grew up in were incredible times in this country. Change and growth and expansion and multiple genres of music happening because of the diversity in our country.

"Knowing which artist should do a song, that's something you learn. And a lot of luck is involved. But the majority of hit songs that come and go have to do with the times, and Lamar had a keen sense of that.

"Lamar had a great sense of humor. Lamar was a pallbearer at Elvis' funeral, and when he was carrying the casket, a tree limb came down and hit him on the back of the head. He looked up and said, 'Are you ever gonna leave me alone?!'

"That's how close a bond Lamar and Elvis had."

* * *

JERRY CHESNUT: "Lamar had his office across from mine on Nashville's Music Row, and we enjoyed a daily friendship for several years. In 1973 he took a song to Elvis I'd written with Billy Edd Wheeler — It's Midnight — and it was the next Elvis single. Elvis liked that song so much that whenever he recorded again later, he always called Lamar and asked, "Let's see what Jerry's got." Thanks to Lamar, Elvis wound up releasing six of my songs including T-R-O-U-B-L-E, Love Coming Down and Never Again.

"When Elvis touched your life, it changed. After he cut It's Midnight, I began not just wanting to write hit songs … I wanted to write Great Songs. Many great things in my life would never have happened without Lamar Fike. I was and will be forever grateful for our association and friendship."

* * *

KENNY DAVIS: "I and my band Mountain Smoke were honored to have Lamar hear us play in Dallas a few years ago. He and Tommy McDonald seemed to enjoy our show. If Lamar liked you, that meant you must be pretty decent!

"In fact, Tom said that Lamar had some very nice things to say about us. He also related that Lamar wanted to help us in any way he could ... but not long after that, his health began to fail. I'm sure if anyone could help a music career it would have been Lamar!

"My proudest moment was receiving a FedEx package nearly seven years ago today. I recognized the address but didn't have a clue what it could be.

"I got the shock of my life when inside I found my Honorary Memphis Mafia membership certificate signed by Lamar! That's something that I will never forget."

* * *

MARY JANE ELLER: "Lamar was my brother, and he was five years older than I was. We were taught to love each other, and we did. We were family and never forgot that fact. I was very proud of Lamar working with Elvis. The status of working for someone so famous wasn't the main reason for my pride. He and Elvis found each other at the perfect time in both of their lives. They were good friends for many years, and they were good for each other. Lamar and Elvis took care of each other. Their lifestyles, backgrounds and interests meshed very well together.

"I always believed that Lamar took the responsibility of caring for Elvis very seriously. He took pride in his work and their relationship. Lamar felt very close to him almost as if he were family. In many ways, they were family. Being only 10 months apart in age, Lamar and Elvis spent their teenage years and grew into adults together. They shared so much with each other.

"Lamar was genuine. He had a quick wit, cleverly wicked sense of humor and, most of all, a big heart. He made friends easily and was kind to most people. Even though Lamar was a big guy physically, he didn't have the heart of a bodyguard. He was a teddy bear in many respects. Lamar lived large, had fun and remembered what was important to him. Lamar remained himself to the end. He was my brother, and I miss him."

* * *

EDDIE KILROY: "I met Lamar in 1962. I had a morning show on the number one pop radio station in Nashville. Lamar came in to bring me a Brenda Lee record. On first meeting, he was very striking. He was very personable with a harmless, sarcastic humor and a sharp mind. Over the years I saw him quite a lot, and I can say this for a fact: there was only one Lamar Fike. He had his own personality, and it was a great personality. I loved him.

"He also had an incredible emotional depth. August 15, 1977, was two days before Elvis was set to begin his New England tour. That morning, Lamar and I were together in Los Angeles at the Intercontinental Hotel. At the time, I was President of Playboy Records, and Lamar and I had finished up signing Lamar's client, Little David Wilkins, to the label. Lamar was getting ready to fly out of L.A. to Portland, Maine, to do the advance work for Elvis' concert on the 17th.

"Lamar came down to my room for some breakfast, and we sat there awhile till all of a sudden he said, 'I need to call the house', meaning Graceland. He dialed out and got someone there on the line. I just listened, and it was clear he was very concerned about Elvis' physical shape. 'Kilroy,' he said, 'Elvis isn't going to make this date.'

"'Oh, sure he will,' I said. Anybody who's worked with temperamental performers know they have their ups and downs.

"But Lamar insisted. Over and over he said, 'I'm telling you, Elvis is not going to make this date.'

"I figured it was just Lamar being dramatic. We went to the airport, and when Lamar exited the car, he turned around and came back. He opened the door and started on again that Elvis wasn't going to make either the Portland concert or even the tour. Finally, he got on the plane, and I flew to Nashville a few hours later.

"Early next morning, the 16th, I went to my office, and my secretary said, 'Lamar Fike is on the phone, and he sounds funny.'

"I took the call, and Lamar was frantic, 'I told you, Elvis is dead! I told you he wouldn't make the tour. Elvis is dead!'

"The news about Elvis' death was just starting to get around through radio and television. I hadn't heard anything yet till Lamar called.

"He had foreseen this day, and now it had come to pass."

* * *

NANCEE (GIBSON) MARGISON: "My loyal and trusted friendship with Lamar Fike began on a flight I was working as a flight attendant between Memphis and Nashville in the 1960s. We remained in touch until his passing. Because of Lamar, I was invited to travel on Elvis' aircraft and attend many shows. Lamar was one of the kindest people I have ever met. I admired his friendship with Elvis, and it was easy to see the feelings were mutual. Elvis was a prankster, and Lamar could give it right back. They were brothers for sure. I remember Elvis telling me that he could not do this without Lamar. I was so proud of my friend and I miss him very much."

* * *

TOMMY McDONALD: "The first time I met Elvis was in 1958 when Lamar invited me to where Elvis and his family were living near Fort Hood. It was right after Gladys Presley had died, and I had my new baby daughter, Dawn, with me, just about 10 weeks old. Everyone was passing her around like a loaf of bread fresh out of the oven, which is to say, 'very carefully', as we were having coffee and pieces of a chocolate cake Elvis' grandmother had baked. All the while outside about 200 local girls were congregated around the house, trying to get a glimpse of Private Presley. It was quite a scene my cousin had introduced me to.

"Years later, at an Elvis concert in Fort Worth in 1975, Lamar, I and Linda Thompson re-acquainted Dawn with Elvis, who could not believe this once-upon-a-time infant was about to graduate from high school. My youngest daughter Dana was in West Virginia and could not attend this particular concert.

"Elvis and Dawn visited for a few minutes, and I stepped back out to the bottom of the stage area when Lamar told me Elvis wanted me to go with him up the backstage steps as he went on to start the show. About half way up the steps, he turned to me and said, 'Tommy, ain't this a hell of way to make a living?' He laughed heartily and went out to thunderous applause.

164

"As the show progressed I was standing by the stage with Linda Thompson, and Elvis was singing one of his beautiful ballads. When the orchestra was playing very softly, I thought that I heard a soft voice speak to me almost like the Lord, a voice that whispered 'Tommy' … I turned to Linda and said, 'Did you hear that whisper?' She smiled at me, and said, 'Tommy, look at Elvis looking down at you and laughing.' I looked at him while I was smiling, shaking my head saying, 'You got me good, this time, Elvis!'

"That love of pranks was one of the qualities that drew Elvis and Lamar together. But the King of Rock 'n' Roll had a serious side as well.

"Once in Las Vegas, just after he had put on a terrific show at the Hilton, Elvis, Lamar, Linda Thompson, Red West, Sonny West and I were passing through the ballroom. Elvis took me aside and said, 'Tommy, come with me. I want to show you something from tonight's show.' We went back onstage and stopped just a few steps from his reserved booth at the end of the T-head.

"Elvis said, 'We have known each other for maybe 15 years. But, Tommy, I never really knew until tonight that you really enjoyed my music.'

"I said, 'Elvis, surely, you jest, sir! I have been a loyal fan of yours since Lamar and I first heard you.'

"'No,' he insisted. 'When I saw you really enjoying the show, I felt real happy about that.'

"People often think a superstar doesn't notice how members of the audience react, but they do, and those reactions in the case of Elvis were taken to heart.

"We went back to the penthouse suite, with everyone relaxing, when Elvis came in with Jackie Wilson, the great R&B artist. Elvis sat down at the piano and started playing, and the two of them started singing. Then Charlie Hodge came in and spelled Elvis at the piano, and a half hour later the suite door opened and in strolled J.D. Sumner with the Stamps behind him. It was an instant Gospel Music Party.

"At the end of the night, Elvis waved to Lamar and me to stay for a minute or so. Elvis said, "Tommy, Lamar says you have to leave in the morning, but I want you to stay for two more days." I had to get back home for business commitments, but Elvis offered to fly me and Lamar on a private jet to where we needed to go if we would remain with him the extra time. Elvis continued to insist, but logistics proved impossible.

"All in all, it showed the lengths Elvis would go to keep close friends around him. Friendship meant a lot to him."

* * *

CHARLES THOMAS ROGERS: "I knew Lamar during our high school days. My best memories of Lamar are very positive. He was fun to be around. He joked a lot, was always upbeat and filled with plans.

"The first time I saw Elvis Presley was in November, 1955, at the Rio Palm Isle, a night club near Kilgore, Texas, that at the time featured talented entertainers working with the *Louisiana Hayride*. I went with a couple of friends, and we had a stage front table. In the corner at the front of the stage, there was a cigar type box for any tips.

"Elvis was dressed in a pink suit, dark turtle neck shirt and dark suede shoes. He introduced himself and his band. It seemed Elvis had a slight stuttering problem; his bass player playfully stood behind him making a winding motion. Elvis started his performance, singing and dancing. His talent captivated the club. No stuttering there!

"On a break, Elvis took us outside to see his pink Cadillac. We sat and talked in the car. He did not drink or smoke, and all of us were about the same age. He told us he would return in two weeks for another performance; very seriously, he asked us to return, which we did. He was such a nice, friendly person."

166

PAT ROLFE: "Lamar was the definition of a trailblazer. The music industry in Nashville was small and wide open in the 1960s and '70s. It was a wonderful period with all kinds of camaraderie. Lamar was a big part of that. To succeed in music publishing, you had to have a good ear for songs, and you had to build and keep your relationships. Lamar had both those qualities. If you were his friend, you were his friend. He couldn't stay mad at anybody."

* * *

BILL SPARKMAN: "My relationship with Lamar Fike began January 8, 1976, when Lamar and his cousin, Tommy McDonald, invited me to join Elvis and his entourage for The King's 41st birthday celebration in Vail, Colorado. During the next 35 years, Lamar introduced me to the powers of the music business, the visionaries who made music happen throughout the world.

"Lamar opened doors for me that no one in the world could have done. I had been writing songs for several years and had signed with Lamar and Tommy to be my publishers. They invited me to come to Nashville and record some of my original songs at Dolly Parton and Porter Wagoner's Fireside Studio. An amazing day followed, supported by Little David Wilkins mixing and directing the session, with his band backing up my music. Along for that session was Elvis' piano player and future president of MCA Records, Tony Brown, and Charley Pride's legendary steel guitar player, Gene O'Neal. Everyone in the studio breathed together that day, and they turned my very simple songs into a wonderful production.

"Lamar, with Tommy McDonald always at his side, provided me the opportunity to realize and participate in a dream that few people can ever realize. My life changed the very minute I met Lamar Fike. I'm delighted his story is now being told."

* * *

LITTLE DAVID WILKINS: "Lamar was not only my manager and mentor, but he was my true friend, introduced to me by Jerry Chesnut. He was a great manager and would go on tour with the band; traveling all those miles in the bus we became like brothers, and even after our management contract expired we stayed closer than brothers. Lamar was a very intelligent man and knew everything that was going on in the world, which amazed me every day.

"Lamar and I loved to eat, so I would take him down to my farm in Parsons, Tennessee, and my mother would cook what Lamar called 'cat head biscuits', plus all the foods Lamar loved, since she was a great Country cook. Lamar could eat the hottest green peppers I've ever seen anyone eat and not breathe fire, so my mother would raise the hottest peppers anyone could grow, then can boxes of them every year just for Lamar.

"My greatest memory is talking to Lamar for at least one hour on the phone a couple of weeks before his death. He said to me, 'I'll be waiting for you when you get here.' He never mentioned where he would be waiting, but I can hardly wait to see him again. I'm sure he will be trying to make a deal on something. I'll love and miss him forever, and I expect him to be waiting on me just like he said he would."

* * *

ANITA WOOD: "In 1957 in Memphis I was co-hosting the *Top 10 Dance Party* with Wink Martindale every Saturday afternoon on local television. One Saturday at the end of the show, Lamar called me and said, 'This is Lamar Fike, and I'm calling for Elvis Presley. Elvis would like to have a date with you this evening.'

"I already had a date, so I couldn't accept and told him so. And Lamar said, 'Are you crazy?! Elvis is asking you out!' I said, 'I'm so sorry, but I can't go.' I thought, well, that's the end of it, I'll never hear from Elvis again.

"A week later, Lamar called again. 'Elvis wants to know if you're free tonight?' And that night I was free, so I said, 'Yes, but he'll have to pick me up.'

"I dated Elvis for about five years and saw Lamar about every time I saw Elvis. He was humorous and so was Elvis, and they were so funny together. They kept me in stitches all the time.

"Lamar was Elvis' right-hand man. Whatever Elvis needed done, Lamar did. He was always loyal to Elvis, like a member of the family. Part of his loyalty came from the fact that Lamar was a big fan of Elvis' music, to begin with. He liked people and the show business atmosphere. I always liked him because he was funny and he was loyal. He was real close to Elvis, a good friend."

* * *

Sharing a ride on Elvis' private plane:
Nancee Margison and Lamar Fike.
(photo courtesy Estate of Lamar Fike)

~ <u>A</u> <u>Family</u> <u>Perspective</u> ~

by Tommy McDonald

There are many memories about my cousin, Lamar Rielly Fike, that come into focus as I write this. Memories growing up between Mart, Texas, Cleveland, Mississippi and Memphis, Tennessee. Our roots in and of these towns are deeply rooted in our Southern Heritage, Christian Faith and in our hearts and minds and souls.

Quite often Lamar would speak with Elvis about our families, concerning both the heartaches and the great times with family closeness, religion and family values. They would talk about Elvis and his cousin, Billy Smith, and Lamar and I as Lamar's cousin, and they would laugh at how our times of growing up were quite startlingly similar.

Lamar's mother, Margaret, and my mother, Velma, were sisters from Mart, Texas. Lamar's mother and Elvis' mother, Gladys Presley, became friends when Lamar was in residence in Graceland in the late 1950s. All three of these ladies were the glue and cement and dominance that perpetuated our families. There was a lot of love and caring that went into all these family relationships.

Lamar was always interested in music. One of our uncles, Doc Stafford, D.D.S., told him, "Lamar, when you were born, the doctor vaccinated you with a Victrola needle." My dad, Glen McDonald, D.D.S., laughed so hard he had tears in his eyes.

Many that knew Lamar did not know he had a very good singing voice and sang in the St. John's Episcopal Church Choir in Memphis. The choir and the church itself made a beautiful combination together, into which Lamar fit quite nicely. Lamar told me that Gladys Presley also had a very nice voice for singing, as she, Elvis and Lamar would often gather around the piano in Graceland and sing together.

170

Both the Elvis Presley family and the family of Lamar Fike moved from Mississippi to Memphis in the same month. So the parallel begins, even though Elvis and Lamar never met until 1954 through Sam Phillips at Sun Records in Memphis.

There were other portents.

Circa 1947-1948, Lamar's father, James, attended a farm implement convention in Chicago and brought the family with him. One evening the family was having dinner in their hotel where Frank Sinatra was entertaining, and Lamar's mother decided she wanted her teenage son to meet Sinatra. James spoke with the people who owned the hotel, and they arranged for the family to go backstage and meet Ol' Blue Eyes after the show. Years later in Hollywood with Elvis, Lamar reminded Frank of that evening, and Frank told Lamar that he certainly did remember that night.

Thinking back to either 1951 or 1952, Lamar and I were in his family home on Philwood Avenue in Memphis one summer afternoon when the doorbell rang. Lamar answered the door, and it was the great gospel bass singer J.D. Sumner, who lived fairly close by. We visited for quite a while, as Lamar had, through the course of his band booking business, met J.D.

At the time Mr. Sumner performed with the The Blackwoods, a leading gospel group whose Memphis concerts were eagerly attended by 16-year-old aspiring gospel singer, Elvis Presley.

Fast forward to June 16, 1954, the parallel resumes as Lamar's father passed away of a massive heart attack in Sikeston, Missouri. Totally devastated, the Fike family moved back to Central Texas. Lamar, however, stayed in Memphis and began learning the rudiments of radio announcing from Dewey Phillips, the deejay who would play Elvis' first commercial record. Lamar also spent time at Sam Phillips' Memphis recording studio during this time, where he first met Elvis.

After a short stint as a deejay at a radio station in Jacksonville, Texas, Lamar was at his mother's home and heard a radio report of Elvis swallowing a cap off of his tooth.

Impulsively, he called the hospital; much to his surprise, Elvis answered the phone in his room and they spoke for a while, until Elvis said, "Well, Lamar, what are you going to do now?"

Lamar replied he did not know, to which Elvis said, "I know what you are going to do. Get in the Chevy, drive straight through to L.A. and come to the studio where I am making a movie."

And that's exactly what Lamar did. When he arrived, Elvis informed him that he would have a role in *Jailhouse Rock*. The next morning Lamar was on the set, putting in motion a work and friendship bond that would last another two decades.

The friendship between the two young men extended to their families. As related to me by my Aunt Margaret, Lamar's mother, and by what Lamar had told me personally, young Lamar was readily accepted by Elvis' mother, Gladys, as a virtual Presley family member.

During the 1957 Christmas season, Lamar's mother, Margaret, was invited to Graceland to spend time with Elvis, Gladys and Vernon, Elvis' grandmother Minnie Mae Presley and Lamar, then living with Elvis' family in Graceland.

In thinking back about that Holiday visit with both families present, I feel that both Gladys and Margaret were of the same opinion that their sons were the most important parts of their lives. I personally feel that Gladys looked upon Lamar as an embodiment of her stillborn son, Elvis' twin. I personally know how much Lamar loved and cared for Gladys, as we had numerous discussions concerning the closeness of their relationship.

My Aunt Margaret (AKA "General Patton", as she was referred to by both our families) was seriously funny. Lamar told me that during the Christmas Dinner at Graceland that year, she looked across the table at Elvis and stared straight into his eyes. "Elvis, you are a very fortunate young man to have my son Lamar caring for and working with you. Do you know and realize that?"

To which Elvis smiled and replied, "Yes, ma'am, Mrs. Fike, I certainly do know that. And I agree with you completely."

And that about said it all.

The following year, 1958, Gladys Presley died in Memphis while Elvis and Lamar were at Fort Hood during Elvis' basic training. After the funeral, Elvis, Lamar and other Presley family members returned to the base; Lamar called me to visit, and that was the first time I met Elvis, along with his grandmother Minnie Mae, dad Vernon, girlfriend Anita Wood and high school friend Red West.

Lamar was adamant that Elvis never had a true time to grieve for his mother before he had to ship out to Germany. From what I saw, I could and would tell you that this 23-year-old young man was really hurting, and I felt very sorry for Elvis and his family.

As Elvis was grieving greatly for the passing of his dear mother, Lamar was silently grieving with him while remembering the sudden passing of his own dear father four years earlier. Elvis and Lamar were both pulled closer to each other ... bonded by the family grief which formed a stronger tie for both men in their understanding and closeness with each other.

That grief would have a singular and unforgettable echo 19 years later. Two days before Elvis died, Lamar had called me from Los Angeles to express his grave concern for Elvis' health and ability to get through the upcoming tour.

Even so, the news of August 16, 1977 was a shock for which no one could properly prepare.

Lamar called me after he arrived back at Graceland from Maine and was understandably upset. "I have hit a solid brick wall," he said. "I have been with Elvis for so many years, and that is all I have lived and breathed and known. For the first time in my life, I feel absolutely alone."

The suddenness of Elvis' death surely hit Lamar as hard as his dad's demise decades earlier. But as he had done then, he again girded himself with the healing power of music, devoting the rest of his days to upholding the legacy of his friend, Elvis Presley.

As we conclude these recollections of my cuz for posterity, I make this very truthful statement: Lamar and I had our family disagreement sessions as a family usually does, but we were always there for each other as Christian families do. In 2006, he bought a house just a block away from us in Arlington, Texas, and the last years of his life were as comfortable as we all could make them for him. He was still enjoying his life until the very end.

I was with Lamar until the monitors flatlined in the Intensive Care Unit at Arlington Memorial Hospital. He did not pass away from cancer, as he had been in remission for three years plus; the official death certificate clearly states the cause of death was sepsis. He would definitely want to make certain that this sort of information was accurate and factual — a trait always prevalent for anyone he had contact with for either personal or business associations.

So, Lamar Rielly, my brother, cuz and confidant, I, we, The Band of Brothers all send our love and affection for you and your talents, accomplishments and personality.

We all know how much you loved and cared for Elvis Aaron Presley from the start to the finish of your travel with him on down Elvis Presley Boulevard.

You truly exemplified the United States Marine Corps motto, "Semper Fi" — "Always Faithful".

As the song says, my man, my brother, "Go rest on high on that mountain in peace" .

* * *

The Fike Family, 3567 Philwood Avenue, Memphis, 1949, the year Lamar began booking local bands. (l-r) James Fike, Margaret Fike, Mary Jane Fike, Lamar Fike.
(photo courtesy Estate of Lamar Fike)

Arlington, Texas, 2001. (l-r) Karen McDonald, Tommy McDonald, Sheila Sparkman, Lamar Fike, Bill Sparkman.
(photo courtesy Estate of Lamar Fike)

~ Riding in the Back Seat of a Tsunami: Recollections of My 35-Year Friendship with Lamar Fike ~

by Bill Sparkman

My life changed even before I met Lamar Fike face to face.

For one or two years before that meeting, I had talked to Lamar over the phone, prompted by his cousin and my very close friend from the early 1970s, Tommy McDonald. During those phone conversations with Lamar, he took me into the exciting life he lived, both on the road and at home with Elvis Presley. Lamar could paint huge mental murals in my brain of the life I longed for in the entertainment industry.

But the very minute I met Lamar in person, he unselfishly allowed me to become a small background proponent of the tsunami called Elvis Presley.

I'm delighted that this book is now telling Lamar's story to the world. A unique and unselfish adventurer living in a "dream" world that just got bigger and bigger in time — and suddenly ended.

I hope my memories of the very exciting events in which Lamar allowed me to participate will help the reader better understand what life in the entertainment world was like during an important time in its history, when music genres were all merging into each other, and the magic concoction became its own self-generating energy source.

My friendship with Lamar lasted until his death in 2011, but the events and memories of those 35 years in between impacted my life powerfully and will remain with me forever. I want to clarify at this time that my observations shared here are about my friend Lamar. While I was provided access to Lamar's world, including a small amount of his time with Elvis, I was not an insider in that world, where the tightly-knit players — the Memphis Mafia — lived, breathed and danced this thing called Life together.

I was only a pilgrim in search of insight and adventure, and because that was what I sought, that is what Lamar gave me. A backseat ride on a tsunami called Elvis Presley.

But when the ride abruptly ended in 1977, my friendship with Lamar lasted another 33 years, and that's when I flourished in my pilgrim's quest.

My first "official" meeting with Lamar occurred on January 8, 1976, in Vail, Colorado. It was Elvis Presley's 41st birthday!

Lamar and Tommy McDonald invited me to join Elvis and his entourage in what would become an "unrestricted" 72-hour adventure in honor of Elvis. With that invitation, a life adventure was about to begin for me.

Tommy and I were at a cardiovascular meeting in Denver and during a break in the final presentations, he pulled me aside and asked, "What are you doing this weekend?"

To which I replied, "Nothing."

Tommy then explained to me that he had just talked to his cousin Lamar, who had flown into Denver with the Memphis Mafia to celebrate Elvis' 41st Birthday in Vail. When Lamar discovered Tommy was in Denver also, he told Elvis, who in turn told Lamar to invite Tommy to join the entourage in Vail.

I didn't hesitate to accept the invitation. Within hours we had confirmed our arrival in Vail with Lamar, with a slight change in our itinerary. Elvis told Lamar to make sure that before we drove to Vail, he wanted us to go to Stapleton Airport, which was the

Denver airport at that time, and receive a guided tour of his airplane, *The Lisa Marie*, which he had just had remodeled.

When we arrived at the Stapleton Airport private plane park, Elvis' pilot, Elwood, was waiting on us. To me, an Elvis fan since I was a boy, this was like ascending the staircase into Air Force One.

I had been in large aircraft before, but when we walked into the plane, the interior looked like a luxury hotel suite with wings. Elwood provided us an insightful tour of the plane, and our visit on *The Lisa Marie* became the ultimate beginning to the weekend that I will never forget.

As we checked into the hotel in Vail, we were met by Lamar and Charlie Hodge and told that Elvis was already enjoying his birthday in the beautiful mountains surrounding Vail. Over the course of the weekend, Elvis bought Cadillacs and Lincoln Continentals for his very close friends. I can't remember the exact number, but I believe it was 14 cars in all. The news media thoroughly enjoyed printing that story in the days to follow.

Lamar had provided Tommy and me a once in a lifetime opportunity to participate in the ELVIS PRESLEY LEGEND. Sadly, not even two years after his Vail birthday celebration, Elvis would be gone.

The weekend ended as quickly as it had begun, but during the next 19 months, Lamar, Tommy and I were on the phone all the time discussing Elvis' adventures and concerts, the exciting life that was occurring daily with this superstar entertainer.

It was during that time that Tommy called me and said Lamar had invited both of us to join the Elvis entourage at an upcoming concert in Dallas, where I would receive and wear one of the coveted Elvis Back Stage Passes. Another exciting adventure awaited me.

That weekend Tommy and I spent time with Elvis' band, bodyguards and backup singers in the hotel. Just before the concert was about to begin, all the invited guests and entourage members boarded the bus that would take us to the auditorium and concert.

I was one of the first people on the bus because I wanted to ensure I didn't miss the excitement I knew lay ahead that night. I wasn't prepared for what I was about to experience.

The buses arrived at the auditorium; we all filed off and were led to an area to await the timed arrival of Elvis' limousine. It arrived exactly as scheduled, and it became obvious to me that the Elvis Business Machine was thoroughly timed and choreographed to run smoothly, from booking the concert to its culmination, including packing everything up after the show and starting the whole cycle over again. The entire experience had been practiced in "real time" for years and worked like a finely-made clock.

People have asked me, "Did you meet Elvis?" I've thought about that answer many times and have come to this conclusion: Yes, I did.

But perhaps not in the way many would be able to understand. So here is a more detailed description of that "meet".

Lamar and Elvis had become as close as adopted brothers, but even with that close relationship, Elvis wanted to know everyone who surrounded him, especially when his concerts were occurring. Which leads to the night that I did meet Elvis, before the concert, for a brief moment.

When Elvis left his limousine, Lamar and the body guards formed around him and proceeded past Tommy and me. Lamar whispered something in Elvis' ear and pointed at me standing with Tommy.

Elvis stopped and smiled at me; he gave me a simple wave of "welcome" with his hand, acknowledging that he was satisfied with Lamar's brief overview of who I was and my character.

I can't imagine what Lamar said to him, but whatever it was, it satisfied him. That warm smile and wave to me was his approval of my presence and his trust in Lamar's judgment.

Then Elvis proceeded past all the well-wishers with Back Stage Passes invited to see the concert in the roped-off VIP area and went into his designated spot by the stage to relax before stepping on stage.

Those of us invited into the VIP area proceeded to the main auditorium. As we entered, something extraordinary occurred as I gazed upon the thousands of fans attending the King of Rock 'n' Roll's performance that night.

AN ELECTRICAL ENERGY FIELD RAN THROUGHOUT MY BODY WHICH I HAD NEVER KNOWN BEFORE, NOR I DOUBT, EVER WILL OCCUR AGAIN! ELVIS PRESLEY'S ARRIVAL IN THE AUDITORIUM WAS UNCHAINED ENERGY, AND THAT EVENING, I FELT THE IMMENSE POWER BEING GENERATED BY HIS FANS AWAITING THE PERFORMANCE THEY WERE ABOUT TO SEE!

When everyone except Elvis had taken their places on stage, Elvis' official concert introduction sounded, the theme from *2001: A Space Odyssey* ... as the crescendo got louder heralding Elvis' entry on the stage, the audience erupted in massive applause as the theme music subsided, and the loud drumming of Ronnie Tutt and the brass instruments began.

At the planned time in the music, Elvis emerged from behind the stage with his bodyguards; walking quickly around the stage, he paused in front of the VIP section and spotted Tommy ... for a split second, he smiled and pointed at him, and then the show began.

As I stood there surrounded by the exciting electricity, it occurred to me that Elvis, Lamar, Tommy and most of the people in the Elvis Entourage had come a long way from the small country towns where our lives began.

As the concert that night came to a close, the Elvis theme music began again, and Elvis left the stage first, followed by the band and singers with the familiar "Elvis Has Left the Building" announced over the speaker system. Just like the choreographed arrival to the auditorium, the departure was a well-oiled machine.

As Tommy and I began to walk past the stage, we heard the voice of The Sweet Inspirations singer Myrna Smith, who had spent time with us earlier that day. "Are you boys going to escort me to the bus?"

We delighted in helping her offstage and walking with her to the bus. After a short ride, we arrived at the hotel where we had originally gathered and marveled at the adventure we had witnessed. And, though the excitement had ended for the invited guests, the Elvis concert personnel were already busy preparing the movement of instruments and sound systems to the next city and venue.

I can't even imagine the excitement that Lamar Fike lived during his 23 years with Elvis. I wonder how he must have felt knowing he was one of the few people in the entire world Elvis fully trusted.

It was a long and trusted friendship that ran full throttle, from Elvis' musical breakout in the Summer of 1954 all the way up to August 16, 1977, when abruptly, like a train locomotive valve opening and the steam from the engine evacuating — at first a loud whoosh, then a fading whisper and finally, absolute quiet as the fire burns out and the energy powering the locomotive is extinguished.

On that dark day, I was in Salt Lake City on business when my pager went off. Seeing Tommy's number on the pager, I immediately called him.

When he answered, he simply asked, "Have you heard the news? Elvis is dead!"

I was shocked! Later that day, I was able to contact Lamar on the phone. His voice was solemn, and I limited the call knowing he had so much on his plate at that time. "Let me know if I can do anything for you, Lamar."

He replied, "Thanks. There's nothing anyone can do now."

The next chapter for Lamar and the other members of the Memphis Mafia, musicians, backup singers and concert crew was about to begin. Lamar and the others who had dedicated their lives to Elvis were left alone. The Dream had ended for them, leaving them all devastated. It was time to turn the page.

After Elvis was buried, Lamar created a publishing and management business in Nashville.

I saw him for the first time after Elvis had died, in Denver, in the spring of 1978, when he was doing a tour with Little David Wilkins, whom he managed at the time.

I vividly remember my first eye-to-eye meeting with Lamar during his visit. I knew from the past that Lamar and Elvis had adopted each other as "brothers" many years prior to Elvis death, and I knew the pain that Lamar had been internalizing since August, 1977.

I hugged him to say hello and could only thank of three words to say to him: "I am sorry!" As we looked into each other's eyes, he became teary-eyed and said a simple, "Thanks." What else could have been said between two friends that would have summed up that moment in time?

Death is such a final event between loved ones, relatives and good friends. Lamar and Elvis' time together ended so quickly and with such force that, retrospectively, I can only imagine the multitude of times Lamar must have spent in total solitude, crying for the loss of his self-adopted brother Elvis.

Lamar must have spent many hours, days, weeks and years playing different scenarios over in his mind … things he wished he had said to Elvis, but somehow, because there seemed so many tomorrows left, the words were never spoken. And tomorrow never came again. Sadness is a lonely place to inhabit.

During that trip to Denver, Lamar gave me another wonderful opportunity. I had been writing songs for several years and had signed with Lamar and Tommy to be my music publishers. During their stop in Denver, Lamar and Tommy invited me to come to Nashville later that year to record some of my songs at Dolly Parton and Porter Wagoner's Fireside Studio.

An amazing day followed, as my recording session unfolded, led by Little David Wilkins mixing and directing the session with his band backing up my music. Along for that session was Tony Brown — Elvis' piano player and future President of MCA Records — and Gene O'Neal, Charley Pride's legendary steel guitar player. Everyone in the studio breathed together that day and turned my very simply written songs into a wonderful production.

Lamar, with Tommy McDonald always at this side, provided me the opportunity to participate in a dream few people can ever realize.

And then, in 2011, I received one of those phone calls no one wants to receive — a call from Tommy with the bad news, "Lamar just died." With that, a long and exciting era in my life came to a close.

During our 35-year friendship, Lamar provided me the ultimate of exciting times. He had allowed me to meet and play music with some of the most accomplished musicians and entertainers in the world's entertainment industry.

Lamar introduced me to the then Power Players of the Music Business, those visionaries who make music happen throughout the world … record producers, songwriters, musicians, performers and recording artists. Lamar opened doors for me that only he could have done.

Before his death, Lamar made me an Honorary Memphis Mafia Member. It's a piece of paper that means more to me than the diplomas I earned.

Lamar generously gave me the education he knew I wanted and did so totally unselfishly for the entire 35 years we knew each other.

I will always be thankful for the close friendships I have had with both Lamar and Tommy, and for Tommy, who has become my "adopted" Brother for what is now over 40 years, including me in what I now have to call, Riding in The Back Seat of a Tsunami.

As Robert Frost concluded in his famous poem, WE TOOK THE ROAD LESS TRAVELED, AND "THAT" HAS MADE ALL THE DIFFERENCE!

I hope that my recollections will help readers get a glimpse of what it was like for a small town boy to participate briefly in a powerful tsunami, and those people who allowed it to happen for me.

Thanks, Lamar.

* * *

~ Special Thanks to Marty Lacker ~

THE McDONALD AND THE FIKE families of Mart, Texas, would personally and respectfully like to thank **Marty Lacker** for his genuine concern, caring, loyalty, comradeship and longtime friendship with our family member "Lamar R. Fike" aka "Cuz".

For those of you that are not aware of what Marty did for his friend, Lamar R. Fike, we would like to tell you about Marty Lacker.

Lamar moved to Arlington, Texas, the last part of May, 2006. From that day forward, Marty faithfully contacted Lamar daily via the phone or e-mails. If Marty could not reach Lamar, he would call me to find out what was going on.

Marty continued this daily with Lamar's trips into the hospital, the rehab center, the short time into the nursing facility and back into the hospital.

If this is not genuine concern, caring, loyalty, comradeship, friendship, then it cannot be defined.

Marty Lacker is definitely an important part in our "We Band of Brothers" family for "Lamar R. Fike".

— *T.S. McDonald*

~ **Meeting Lamar Fike** ~

by Harold F. Eggers, Jr.

In the late 1970s my brother Kevin Eggers hired me to serve as road manager for one of the star performers of his Tomato Records label — legendary singer/songwriter Townes Van Zandt.

Over the next two decades I wore many hats with Townes, eventually becoming his manager and the business partner of his live recordings.

My association with Townes transformed my life in many ways — not the least of which was meeting Lamar Fike, who was then Townes' manager. At that time Lamar and his cousin Tommy McDonald had a management company and booking agency in Nashville, and Townes was one of their many notable clients.

In 1997 Townes passed away. At his funeral in Nashville, I encountered Lamar, speaking with him for some time. Instinctively, he saw I was in bad shape with the loss of my friend, and he suggested I come by his home the next day to advise me on what the future held for me, now that I would no longer be working and touring with Townes.

Lamar, of course, had been down that long, lonesome road before.

He told me his world had been shattered the day Elvis died. It had taken years, he said, to put back the pieces. Even in the present, Lamar averred, Elvis remained a daily presence in his thoughts.

I will never forget the compassion, understanding and advice Lamar gave me that day. He also shared his personal contact information, letting me know I was welcome to call anytime to discuss what we had talked about and more.

During the next few years, I frequently took him up on this offer and spoke often on the phone. Occasionally, fascinating snippets of Lamar's time with Elvis would pop into the conversation — living at Graceland and enjoying late nights with Elvis singing and playing gospel piano, while Gladys Presley and Lamar harmonized in the background ... singing with Elvis backstage before a show to help the King of Rock 'n' Roll warm up his vocal cords ... the serious task of introducing new songwriters to keep Elvis' recorded repertoire at peak level.

One day, I was struck by a powerful thought: perhaps Lamar would want to set down in a book his memories from 23 years with the world's greatest musical superstar.

I contacted Lamar about the idea of myself and music writer L.E. McCullough sitting with him for an extended series of interviews about his closest friend, Elvis Presley. Lamar was immediately receptive, and after a year of schedule-shifting to find the right time and place for the three of us to convene, L.E. and I were graciously welcomed into Lamar's Nashville home.

The concept for the book was simple: ask Lamar short, basic questions about Elvis and record his short, to-the-point answers. What resulted was a treasure trove of anecdotes and insights that encompassed the vast universe of Elvis truth, myth and beyond.

We worked on the book with Lamar up until his death. I spoke with Lamar regularly throughout this process. In 2006, Lamar moved from Nashville to Arlington, Texas, to be near his cousin Tommy and his wife Karen McDonald, who looked after Lamar and gave him the best of care, seeing him daily. When Lamar went into the hospital the final time, Tommy was at his side each day.

In November, 2010, I drove from Austin to Arlington to see Lamar in the hospital. We spoke of how we would publicize this book and other Elvis-themed books we would create via podcasts, video documentaries, book tours and more. Lamar never tired of talking about Elvis and about Elvis' impact on shaping the world we live in today. It was clear they had been as close as brothers can possibly be.

Lamar passed away January 21, 2011, before he could see the publication of *Elvis: Truth, Myth & Beyond*. I was invited to speak at his funeral and was astounded at the outpouring of affection and respect for this unassuming individual who had encouraged and assisted so many people to hone their talents and believe in their dreams.

Including me.

I will always remember Lamar Fike as one of the grandest of characters I have ever known. Through this book, you will have gotten to know him a little bit, too.

Of course, you won't learn <u>everything</u> about him or his great friend Elvis … keeping a little bit of mystery in the mix is how they'd probably like it.

* * *

Final resting place, Mart, Texas.
(photo courtesy Estate of Lamar Fike)

~ **The Authors** ~

L.E. McCULLOUGH is a native of Speedway, Indiana, and has worked as a journalist, musicologist, script and stage writer with 49 books published in fiction, non-fiction, drama, essay and audiobook fields. He has published hundreds of articles on music and the music industry in *Billboard*, *Vista*, *Living Blues*, *Singout*, *Texas Highways*, *Goldmine*, *La Prensa*, *New Groves Dictionary of Music in the U.S.* and served as music columnist for *Austin American-Statesman*, *Austin Chronicle*, *901 Magazine* and *Music Row*. His stage play on legendary blues pianist Leroy Carr, *Blues for Miss Buttercup*, debuted in New York City in June, 1995, and won the Urban Stages Emerging Playwrights Award. Dr. McCullough holds a Ph.D. in ethnomusicology from the University of Pittsburgh. **www.lemccullough.com**

* * *

HAROLD F. EGGERS, JR. of Austin, Texas, is a music industry executive of 40 years' experience who first met Lamar Fike when he and Mr. Fike were working with legendary singer/songwriter Townes Van Zandt. Mr. Eggers worked with Van Zandt for 20 years, co-owning and co-producing eight Townes Van Zandt albums including the Nashville Nammy-nominated *Road Songs* album that featured a track used in the Coen Brothers' film *The Big Lebowski*. Mr. Eggers also managed Whitey Shafer, a prolific singer/songwriter who wrote numerous chart hits for George Jones, Lefty Frizzell, Merle Haggard, George Strait, Lee Ann Womack, Kenny Chesney and other country stars. Co-owner of Donovan/Eggers Music Publishing & Recordings, Mr. Eggers was the literary manager of record for bringing to publication Susie Nelson's *Heartworn Memories: A Daughter's Personal Biography of Willie Nelson* (Simon & Schuster), *Stevie Ray: Soul to Soul* by Keri Leigh (Taylor) and *The Nashville Family Album* by Alan Mayor (St. Martin's). **www.townesvanzandt20yearshfe.com**

~ **Acknowledgments** ~

* For personal remembrances of Elvis Presley and Lamar Fike:

Ray Baker; Jimmy Bowen; Jerry Chesnut; Kenny Davis; Kevin Eggers;
Mary Jane Eller; Eddie Kilroy; Nancee Margison; Tommy McDonald;
Charles Thomas Rogers; Pat Rolfe; Marla Sanderson;
Bill Sparkman; Little David Wilkins; Anita Wood

* For personal support and friendship through the project:

Lisa Bansavage; Nonie & Bruce Beard; Valerie & Edgar Campbell;
Gary Carpenter; Bobbie Childs; Bill Cook; Guy & Jean Crouch;
Ken Davis, Sr.; Lee Davis; Mardeana Davis; Megan & Tyler East;
Harold & Honora Eggers; Harold F. Eggers-Soo III;
Kevin Eggers; Pat & Dennis Eggers; Jackie & Lanny Fife;
Jim Fox of Silman-James Press; Bud Gillam; Kathleen Hudson, Ph.D.;
Patrick Hurley; Eugene Lamar Johnson, Ph.D.; Kimberly Layne, LAc;
Kathy & Mark Luckadoo; Buddy McDonald & Emma Dell McDonald;
Christopher McDonald; Dana McDonald; Danielle McDonald;
Dawn McDonald; Karen A. McDonald; Dr. S.E.G. McDonald, D.D.S
& Velma McDonald; Morris H. Nelson; Peggy & Stephen Nolan;
Tristen, Eva & Cassidy O'Rear; Leslie, Leslynn, Arissa & Nate Perez;
John W. Post; Jeanne Schillaci, Ph.D.; George Schinler; Tony Seidl;
M.E. Shaw; Dr. Cameron Shropshire, M.D.
& Dr. Susan Moses Shropshire, M.D.; Sylvie Simmons;
Gene Soo; Cynthia Soo; Bill & Sheila Sparkman;
Howard and Evelyn Thompson; Herschel Wells;
Claire and Lynn Williams; Sharon Wills, Ph.D.; Roy Wohleb

* For editorial research assistance:

Linda Bogard of Getty Images;
Raymonde Pozzolano of Words Unlimited;
Toby Silver of Sony Music;
Pam Wertheimer of W Management;
Tishana Williams of Authentic Brands Group

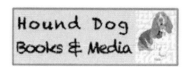